This book can give you new life and direction, and let you start anew with a new attitude.

BANKRUPTCY

SURVIVAL

GUIDE

Xue Tianyu

Bankruptcy survival guide

Xue Tianyu

Front   Words

Dear readers:

I am pleased to share with you the book Surviving Bankruptcy and introduce you to its contents here. Writing this book was a very special experience for me. Because I have experienced the pain of failure in the business world, and experienced the fear of being in debt and running out of money. But now that I'm out of that predicament, I want to share my experience and my journey with you. I hope this book can be a must-have guide in your life.

I am an ordinary person, also once like you, full of ambition and vision, hope to be able to succeed in the business field through their own efforts. However, I have also failed, and I have experienced bankruptcy and the threat of debt, which makes me feel very depressed and helpless. But it was this painful experience that made me realize many of the basic principles of life and success. This book is not only about sharing my experience, but more importantly, it is about helping you move on from failure, discover new opportunities, acquire more skills, and live better.

The purpose of this book is to provide practical and easy-to-follow advice on how to get out of bankruptcy and achieve your dreams. Through my own experiences, case studies, unique perspectives and practical tips, I will teach you how to manage your money better, reduce your expenses, find new opportunities and lifestyles, and set achievable goals. I believe that if you make good use of this information, you will be able to face the future with more confidence, so that failure is just a process in your life.

I wrote this book to help people who have failed, like me, find the courage to start over and help them transform their negativity into a new path. I hope this book can become a superhero in your life and help you further your dreams. I sincerely hope that this book will give you new life and direction, and let you start anew with a new attitude.

Finally, I want to say that I understand your pain, I feel your predicament, but I believe that all this is just the beginning of failure, not the end of life. Believe in yourself, believe in the future. By reading this book, I believe you too can discover and regain the motivation and strength to face the new day.

I wish you success!

Author: Xue Tianyu

Date: March 30, 2023

eye Record

Chapter 1: Facing the Challenge of Failure and Bankruptcy

Causes and background of failure and bankruptcy

Although "broke" may be a disappointing word, a successful life is not just about success-it also requires failure to some extent. Bankruptcy is not an ugly thing. We have all failed before, and the hardships of life only make us stronger. The goal of this book, therefore, is to show that, even in times of failure and bankruptcy, people can find different ways of being happy and surviving through lack of money. In that inevitable period, we need to build resilience in order to start afresh. This section will explore several factors and contexts that lead to personal bankruptcy.

Be defrauded into bankruptcy

Counterfeit drug fraud

Selling fake drugs, defrauding consumers of their money and endangering public health.

Case:

Because Xiao Zhang suffered from a serious illness, he listened to the words of a fake medicine salesman and bought expensive fake medicines. However, these fake drugs did not have any effect, but caused Xiao Zhang's physical condition to become more serious. In the end, Xiao Zhang's medical expenses combined with the loss of buying fake drugs plunged his life into great financial difficulties and even led to bankruptcy.

Xiao Li, who suffers from heart disease, took the advice of a so-called Chinese medicine practitioner and bought a fake medicine that claimed to cure heart disease. However, this fake medicine did not have any effect, but aggravated Xiao Li's illness. At this time, Xiao Li's wife could not afford medical and drug costs, had to sell the family's property, vehicles and other property, ultimately did not save Xiao Li's life.

Xiao Wang's child suffered from severe lung disease and bought a high-priced fake medicine on the advice of a person named "Miracle Doctor". However, the fake medicine didn't work, and Wang had to spend a lot of time and money looking for other treatments. Eventually, Xiao Wang's financial burden became unbearable and he had to go bankrupt. At the same time, his child's condition did not improve.

Card fraud

Obtain other people's card information by means of fraud, theft, duplication, forgery, etc., and illegally transfer money from their accounts.

Case:

Xiao Zhang, a young white-collar worker, plans to buy a computer online, so he enters his bank card information. Soon after, he found that his card had been stolen and swiped tens of thousands of yuan, and his account owed rent for several months. Xiao Zhang tried to contact the bank customer service, but the time and amount of the stolen card could not be determined, he could not provide evidence to sue the thief, eventually, he had to leave the city sadly, bankrupt back home.

When Xiao Li was shopping, he was stared at by an unidentified person. This person took advantage of Xiao Li's inattention and secretly took Xiao Li's wallet, which contained Xiao Li's bank card. Soon after, Xiao Li found that his card had been stolen and swiped tens of thousands of yuan. Unable to pay rent and other expenses, he eventually had to sell his house and, with nowhere to go, chose to live on the streets.

Xiao Wang, recommended by a friend, downloaded an app called "Free Traffic", thinking he could get free network traffic. Unexpectedly, this application is a kind of malware, using Wang input personal information and bank card information for fraud and theft. Xiao Wang's card was stolen and swiped tens of thousands of yuan, and his account was emptied, resulting in his inability to repay, eventually bankruptcy, life in trouble.

SMS fraud

By sending false prizes, bank cards expired and other information, in order to defraud the victim's property.

Case:

Xiao Ming, a college student, received a text message saying he had won a lucky draw in a large supermarket and could get a shopping card of 10,000 yuan. Xiao Ming was very excited, clicked on the link to fill in his personal information and paid a small fee. A week later, he received a fake shopping card, but was deducted 10,000 yuan from his bank card balance. Xiao Ming was so heavily in debt that he was forced to drop out of school and return home.

The retired grandfather received a text message saying that his bank card was about to expire and needed to click on the link to update it.

Grandpa filled in the credit card information according to the prompts, but the credit card bill for the month showed millions of yuan of consumption records, most of which were used for online shopping and investment. Since the old man did not have enough money to pay his debts, his house and savings were forced by the bank.

Young white-collar money received a message saying his bank account had been stolen and needed to click on a link to confirm. Small money not only filled in personal information, but also entered the bank card number and password, then his bank card was immediately transferred tens of thousands of yuan by the swindler. The debt of the small money thus increased, and eventually had to give up the housing deposit and the previously purchased vehicle.

The owner of a small business received a false tender message claiming to be awarded a large engineering contract worth millions of dollars. The boss paid the deposit and contract signing fee according to the prompt in the text message, but no construction project was carried out. As a result, the boss fell into a situation where the capital chain was broken, and had to lay off employees and eventually shut down the enterprise.

Xiao Fang, a primary school student, received a message saying she had won a big prize of 5 million yuan by buying lottery tickets. Xiao Fang was excited, filled in her personal information and paid a handling fee according to the prompts in the text message, but finally did not receive any reward. Xiao Fang's family ran up a lot of debt and had to sell their house and car.

False recruitment fraud

In the name of recruitment, promise high salary, easy work and other unrealistic conditions, lure job seekers to pay a certain fee, but finally do not fulfill the promise.

Case:

Mr. Li saw a high-paying job advertisement published by a game company on the Internet. The company promised job seekers a good salary and a comfortable working environment. Mr. Li paid a deposit of 5000 yuan for the job. However, when he arrived at the company for an interview, he found that the company was just an office in an alley with no sign of game development. Mr. Li's deposit was cheated away, and the job could not be realized. He had to go to the bank to borrow money to make a living.

Miss Zhang saw an advertisement for a foreign trade salesman on the Internet, and the company promised to provide high commissions and generous bonuses. In order to get the job, Miss Zhang paid 10000 yuan as training fee. However, her training was only a lecture that was irrelevant. The company's so-called foreign trade business was just selling some small commodities through Taobao. Ms. Zhang's training fees were useless, but she was scraped away a lot, and she had to rely on her family to help her get by.

Mr. Wang saw an online advertisement for a high-paying community manager posted by a headhunting company, which promised to provide five insurances and one fund and withhold social insurance and housing provident fund. In order to get the job, Mr. Wang paid 2500 yuan in advance for social security and housing accumulation fund. When he went to sign the contract, he found that the company's so-called contract was just a fake contract. After that, the company found various reasons to delay not to pay wages, Mr. Wang's life suddenly became difficult.

investment fraud

In the name of high income, fictitious investment projects, defrauding investors of money.

Case:

Xiao Li saw an investment project on social media that claimed to give him high returns in a short period of time. Xiao Li was attracted and invested all his savings without hesitation. Soon after, the investment project declared bankruptcy, Xiao Li was cheated of all his money, so he went bankrupt.

Xiao Wang was persuaded by a so-called asset management company to invest his pension in the company's investment projects. The company promised high returns and quickly gained Wang's trust. As a result, the company suddenly went bankrupt, and Xiao Wang lost all his pension, couldn't pay his living expenses, and was in financial trouble.

Xiao Zhang took the advice of a stranger and invested all his savings in an investment project called Ponzi. The project claimed to allow him to enjoy medium-to-high returns and attracted a large number of investors.

Unfortunately, however, the investment project was a Ponzi scheme, and Xiao Zhang was cheated of all his money and had to file for bankruptcy.

Internet fraud

Through online chat, social accounts and other means, with all kinds of good temptations and promises to defraud the victim of money.

Case:

Xiao Wang, a company employee, received a friend application on WeChat from a strange woman who claimed to be an investor who helped people manage their finances. Xiao Wang covet convenience, soon added each other's friends, and listened to his investment advice. Before long, Wang began to inject money into the "investor", but later found that his account had no money. It turned out that the "investor" was a swindler. In the process of chatting with Xiao Wang, he constantly let Xiao Wang believe his words through various skills, defrauded a large amount of funds, and finally made Xiao Wang bankrupt.

Xiao Li is a young girl who one day receives a private message on Social networks from a man who claims to be a rich foreigner. The man claimed that he had a lot of wealth and was willing to share some with Xiao Li. So he defrauded her of her property by various promises and threats. In the course of chatting with the man, Xiao Li was tempted by his wealth and luxury, constantly withdrawing cash from his bank account, eventually leading to Xiao Li's bankruptcy.

Xiao Zhang, a young college student, once met a girl on an online blind date and established a relationship. Soon, the girl expressed strong feelings for him and promised to stay with him. But soon after, the girl began to ask Xiao Zhang for all kinds of money and gifts, Xiao Zhang could not bear this burden, but was threatened and blackmailed by the girl. In order to get himself out of this predicament, Xiao Zhang had to transfer a large amount of money from the bank, causing it to fall into bankruptcy. Stealing personal information: stealing the personal information of the victim by means of deception, illegal acquisition, theft, etc., so as to provide means for the lawbreakers to make huge profits from it.

Marketing fraud

Through false propaganda, fabrication of facts and other means to deceive consumers to buy goods or services inconsistent with the promise, from which to obtain huge profits.

Case:

After buying a membership card for a fitness center, Mr. Zhang was told he could get unlimited personal training services and high-end fitness equipment throughout the year. However, after only a few uses, Mr. Zhang found that the fitness center did not provide the promised service, the private teachers were not as professional as they advertised, and the fitness equipment was of poor quality. Eventually, Mr. Zhang was repeatedly asked to buy other packages and value-added services, leading to a deterioration in his financial situation and eventual personal bankruptcy.

Ms. Li was attracted by an online store called "Beauty Shop" during an online purchase. The online store boasts top-notch beauty products that can help Ms. Li realize her beauty dream. However, the products Ms. Li received were found to be of extremely poor quality and had no cosmetic effect at all. In addition, the online store also swiped a large number of cards into the Alipay or WeChat accounts used by the buyers without knowing them, resulting in the misappropriation of Ms. Li's account funds and eventual personal bankruptcy.

Mr. Wang bought an expensive laptop at an electronics supermarket. The salesman promised top performance and quality, and offered a three-year on-site warranty. However, the computer broke down after just a few uses, and Mr. Wang contacted the store and was told that only free remote repair services were available, and that it would take at least half a month to solve the problem. Eventually, Mr. Wang was dismissed by his boss because of delays in data related to the company's work.

routine loan

In the name of high-interest loans, the victim is pushed to the brink of collapse in order to force the victim to repay the loan, which is suspected of extortion.

Case:

Ms. Wang, an elderly person living alone, applied for a high-interest loan online because her family needed some extra expenses. Soon, she was contacted by the routine loan company and told that the loan had been approved. However, the loan company asked Ms. Wang to pay high fees and interest. In desperation, Ms. Wang agreed, but she did not expect that the loan would be her nightmare. The loan company began to force her to repay the loan, and even began to harass Ms. Wang's relatives and friends, eventually leading to her bankruptcy.

Xiao Li is a young man who applied for a loan online because he wanted to buy a house. Soon, a routine loan company contacted him and told him that his loan had been approved. But the loan company asked Xiao Li to pay high interest and security deposit. Although Xiao Li felt wrong, he agreed. But as time went on, Xiao Li found that the loan company's repayment method was extremely bad, and they constantly threatened to tell Xiao Li that if he did not repay, he would be hit. In the end, Xiao Li went bankrupt.

Mr. Zhang is a businessman who needs a loan to expand his business. But because of his poor credit history, the bank rejected his application. Soon, the routine loan company contacted him and told him that his loan had been approved. However, the loan company asked Mr. Zhang to pay high fees and interest. Mr. Zhang thought it was an opportunity, so he agreed. But as time went on, Mr. Zhang discovered that the loan company was a scam. They continued to force Mr. Zhang to repay the loan and even began to harass his clients, eventually leading to Mr. Zhang's bankruptcy.

gambling bankruptcy

Mahjong gambling

Case:

After retirement, Lao Wang became addicted to mahjong and spent a lot of time and money in the mahjong hall every day. He eventually owed high gambling debts and was forced to sell his house and vehicle. His children had to take over the debt and the family was in financial trouble.

Xiao Zhang met a seemingly kind-hearted grandmother in the mahjong hall. The grandmother defrauded Xiao Zhang's money again and again in a tone that winning or losing was not important. In the end, Xiao Zhang was cheated out of much and had to borrow money from family and friends, leading to family breakdown and interpersonal breakdown.

Xiao Li and a group of friends often play in the mahjong hall, winning and losing money, originally just to pass the time and unite feelings. However, in recent months they have encountered a group of gamblers who specialize in scamming novices and repeatedly suppressing Xiao Li and his friends. After several big losses, Xiao Li and his team had to gradually flee the mahjong hall, and the amount of money cheated was increasing, leaving their team falling apart.

After busy work, Wang became addicted to mahjong apps, not only gambling and energy were swallowed up, but he had to lie during work hours and social circles to justify fictional losses. Eventually, his company found out that the director had acted so irresponsibly that he was fired and had little savings to spend because he was in arrears with his daily expenses. Eventually, he had to return to his parents 'home and start a new life.

Poker gambling

Case:

Xiao Ming is a poker fan. He plays poker constantly every day, investing time and money crazily. Because studying poker is too expensive, Xiao Ming has to take out his long-standing savings to play. Eventually, he lost all his savings, lost his job and was saddled with huge debts.

Xiao Hong is a professional poker player who enjoys playing poker on some European betting sites. As she kept losing money, she began to mortgage her house and car to play the game. Eventually, she lost all her collateral and savings and was sued for bankruptcy by the bank.

Mr. Zhang is a middle-aged man, because his job is not satisfactory, he began to play poker to eliminate his stress. He eventually became an obsessive gamer, standing for hours at a time every day, affecting his work and family life. He even ended up with a huge debt, and the family was facing a huge threat.

Xiao Gang is a poker enthusiast who often plays online games. At first he thought of nothing more than taking a little time to see how his luck was, but he became obsessed and soon could not live without playing cards. He gradually lost all his savings in the game and finally had to borrow money from his family, which he was unable to repay and eventually declared bankruptcy.

Lottery gambling

Case:

Xiao Li is a young newcomer to the workplace. He always has fantasies about winning the lottery. In order to try his luck, he began to buy lottery tickets and gradually became addicted to them, buying them every day until he went bankrupt. In the end, Xiao Li exhausted all his savings to pursue those illusory dreams, and he was only a victim of deception.

Mr. Zhang is a middle-aged man who has accumulated a lot of wealth in his career. However, his wealth did not bring him happiness and satisfaction. Instead, he began to buy lottery tickets in pursuit of more happiness. In the end, he lost everything and even put his family at great financial risk.

Xiao Zhang, a college student, had a preliminary success in buying lottery tickets. However, in order to achieve more wealth, he began to invest money continuously. In the end, he not only lost his savings, but also ran up a huge debt that made his life difficult.

Ms. Li is a single mother who is under great pressure between work and family. To relieve her stress, she started buying lottery tickets and indulged in them. Instead of winning the grand prize, however, she lost a significant amount of money, putting her family at even greater financial risk.

Mr. Wang is a businessman who has succeeded in his work and accumulated a lot of wealth. However, he didn't learn how to manage his money and started buying lottery tickets and indulging in them. Eventually, he lost all his savings and investments, bankrupting his business and plunging him into personal ruin.

Internet gambling

Case:

Xiao Ming is a promising young programmer, but his addiction to online gambling made him lose everything. His initial bets were only small amounts of money, but soon he lost control and began to borrow money from loan sharks to continue gambling. His debts grew until they eventually led to his bankruptcy. He lost his job, his family and all his possessions, and now he has nothing but charity to help him live on.

Xiaofang, a girl, has been obsessed with online gambling since college, which she thinks is an easy way to make money. She invested a lot of time and money in it and had some success for quite some time. However, luck eventually failed her, she lost all her savings, and the family was in trouble. In her despair, she had also been deceived. She had been tricked by swindlers in the name of gambling platforms, which eventually led her into a deeper desperate situation.

The man Xiao Li is a successful entrepreneur, but his addiction to online gambling has left him devastated. He spends a lot of time playing online gambling every night, even in the office will find opportunities to brush some online gambling. Eventually, his online gambling debt has reached several million yuan, he had to go bankrupt and close down. He lost all his business assets and personal possessions, as well as his wife and children, and constantly dragged his family to pay his debts.

Addictive consumption bankruptcy

Handmade toy

Case:

Xiao Ming is a post-80s otaku, his room is full of all kinds of cartoon characters. He would spend a lot of money on action figures every month until his savings were all spent. In order to satisfy his desire to buy, he began to borrow money and debt, and eventually went bankrupt.

Xiao Hong is a girl who starts spending wildly because she likes to buy hand-made things. She often buys limited-edition hand-made models online and doesn't even eat or drink to buy them, eventually pushing herself to the brink of bankruptcy.

Mr. Wang is a middle-aged man who is gradually addicted to collecting hand figures. He often spends a lot of money on hand figures, and even family expenses are beginning to suffer. Eventually, his family broke up and he lost his job, which eventually led to bankruptcy.

Xiao Zhang was a student who went bankrupt because he liked to collect figurines. He spent his monthly allowance on action figures and eventually started borrowing money from friends. However, when he got into debt, he couldn't pay his debts and eventually went bankrupt.

Xiao Li is a young woman who is addicted to buying hand-made things. She often went on an online shopping spree, even though she knew her finances were in jeopardy. Eventually, unable to repay the debts she had accumulated over the years, she had to declare bankruptcy and give up her hobby.

Pet bankruptcy

Case:

Xiao Ming is a passionate pet lover who keeps a cat and a dog at home. Because of his love for pets, he keeps buying pet toys, food and medical expenses. These expenses gradually exceeded his budget and he had to borrow money to pay for them. Eventually, Xiao Ming took on huge debts, which led to his bankruptcy.

Lily is a young pet craft designer who makes cute pet toys and costumes in her studio. She has amassed millions of followers on Social networks and is favored by many clients both at home and abroad. However, Lili is too obsessed with pets and creation to pay much attention to financial management. Eventually, her design studio faced bankruptcy due to financial problems.

Xiao Li, a student obsessed with cats, keeps eight cats in his apartment. Because of the increased cost of breeding and feeding, he had to spend a lot of money to feed his cats. However, these expenses gradually exceeded his budget, making it impossible for him to afford his own tuition and daily living expenses. Xiao Li tried to sell his cats to tide him over, but failed to find a buyer and went bankrupt.

Xiao Zhang is a dog owner who has two beautiful Yorkshire terriers. To give his dogs the best possible life, he keeps buying high-end dog food, dog chews, shampoos and health care products. These extra costs gradually built up a financial roadblock that led to his bankruptcy.

Mr. Wang is a wealthy salesman who loves pets. He has a golden retriever and a Persian cat and is committed to providing them with meticulous care and care. However, Mr. Wang neglected to manage his finances and unknowingly spent a lot of money on expensive dog food and pet health supplies. This resulted in his savings account becoming smaller and smaller, and ultimately unable to support his living expenses and other investments to build his assets.

nitrous oxide addiction

Case:

Mr. Li is a young online celebrity who often breathes laughing gas and shares his happy moments on live broadcasts. However, over time, he began to lose control of his addiction to laughing gas and spent a lot of time and money buying it every day. In the end, he not only lost all his savings and fame, but also faced long-term health problems.

Miss Wang, a young professional woman, found that laughing gas could relieve her stress and anxiety. However, as time went on, she began to lose her self-control and spent a lot of time and money buying laughing gas. Eventually, her career suffered because she couldn't concentrate on her work and took frequent breaks.

Mr. Zhang is a young student who thinks laughing gas can help him study and think better. Over time, however, his addiction to laughing gas deepened and he stopped focusing on his studies and social life. Eventually, he lost his studies and relationships to his pursuit of laughing gas.

Mr. Chen is a young entrepreneur who started a new business. However, his addiction to laughing gas prevented him from focusing on his work and eventually led to the company's bankruptcy. He lost all his investments and reputation, and was also heavily in debt.

Miss Wu is a young entertainer who needs to maintain a positive and cheerful image in her work and daily life. Over time, however, her addiction to laughing gas made it impossible for her to maintain stable emotions and focus. Eventually, she lost all her collaborations and fans, and faced irreparable health problems.

Indulge in making friends

Case:

Mr. A is addicted to looking for a girl and spends a lot of money and energy looking for the girl he likes. However, the girls kept extorting money from him, which made him more and more destitute and eventually led to his bankruptcy.

Mr. B neglected the development of his business because he was addicted to finding prostitutes, which led to a decline in the company's performance. In order to make a living and continue to find a lady, he had to mortgage the company's shares, and eventually the company was forced to go bankrupt.

Mr. C is obsessed with finding girls, constantly investing in and doting on girls, and eventually loses a lot. Not only did he use up all his savings, but he also ran up a lot of debt and eventually had to file for bankruptcy.

Mr. D is obsessed with finding prostitutes and spends a lot of money on this activity every day. But he didn't grow in business, eventually languishing in a competitive market and eventually being forced to close the company.

Mr. E lost his plan and vision for the future because he was addicted to looking for girls. After spending a lot of money and energy, he ended up in financial trouble and had to file for bankruptcy to get out of debt.

Business failure, bankruptcy

No market

Case:

A young man is passionate about developing an instant music production software, and he has invested a lot of time and money to develop a perfect product. However, when the product launched the market, he found that the market has been divided by several large companies, the user's demand for new products is relatively small, the market saturation caused his products can not break through, and finally he had to go bankrupt.

After a long period of research and experimentation, a couple have developed a brand new healthy food. They believed that there must be someone in the market who needed this product, so they began commercial production. However, they failed to anticipate the strength of their competitors, and several large companies have taken major market share. Due to lack of market share and publicity, their products could not bring enough benefits to users, and eventually led to bankruptcy.

A young programmer sees the rise of artificial intelligence technology and decides to start his own smart home-related business. He invested all of his time and money to develop a smart home system that performed brilliantly in every way. However, he ignored the severity of the market competition, the lessons of failure, and finally he was forced to go bankrupt in the case of market saturation.

A young man developed a new social platform by analyzing current Social networks and entertainment needs. However, he ignored the monopoly of big companies, and his software could not replace the software that users had become accustomed to. Under the pressure of the market, his company finally went bankrupt.

Lack of funds

Case:

Xiao Ming wants to open a coffee shop, but he doesn't have enough money to rent a good location and buy high-quality coffee beans. Because Xiao Ming's coffee shop is located in a relatively remote location, his income has not been enough to support his rent and supplier fees, and finally had to close his coffee shop.

Xiaohong started a convenience store in a residential area, but she didn't have enough money to maintain her inventory levels. Because her husband lost his job, she had to bear the family expenses herself. For a short time, she failed to make enough profit to pay her suppliers and eventually closed her convenience store.

Xiao Li's startup is an app development team. He and his partners didn't have enough money to hire high-level developers and designers. Despite good potential and market demand for their app, they were unable to properly conduct marketing campaigns due to lack of funds and eventually went bankrupt.

Xiaohua is an independent fitness trainer with the intention of opening her own fitness studio. However, she doesn't have enough money to pay for rent and equipment to compete for a nearby gym. Because she couldn't attract enough customers, her business failed.

Xiao Wang has started a new model association in the university to organize and market model association activities. Because they lack sufficient funds to pay for venue rentals and produce promotional materials, their events are unable to attract enough participants and sponsors. Eventually, they were forced to close their union.

mismanagement

Case:

Xiao Ming started a fast food restaurant, but without proper cost control and price planning, his costs were too high and prices were too low to make a profit, which eventually led to the bankruptcy of his fast food restaurant.

Xiao Hong wanted to open a gift shop, but because she didn't do enough market research and marketing strategy, her store couldn't attract enough consumers, and eventually her gift shop went bankrupt.

Xiao Liu started a hand-made furniture company, but because he did not establish a proper supply chain and production plan, his cost was too high, his output was insufficient, and he could not meet the market demand, which eventually led to the bankruptcy of his furniture company.

Xiao Wang started a pet hospital, but because he didn't have the right financial management and investment plan, he couldn't afford the high medical expenses and equipment costs, which eventually led to the bankruptcy of his pet hospital.

Zhang started a gym, but because he didn't have the right marketing and membership plan, he couldn't attract enough members, pay high rent and staff salaries, and eventually his gym went bankrupt.

Mode error

Case:

A restaurant entrepreneur believes that buying the cheapest ingredients can significantly reduce costs, but ignores the impact of the quality and taste of the ingredients on customers. Eventually, their customers were dissatisfied with the quality and taste of the food, which led to the restaurant's business going downhill and eventually closing down.

An online education startup is dedicated to providing online learning services for students. They intend to live entirely on advertising revenue, with no fees. However, due to the depression of the educational advertising market, the company could not make a profit under the condition of insufficient advertising revenue, and finally went bankrupt.

A retail chain startup decided to expand rapidly without investing in employee training and development. As a result, employees were unable to respond effectively to various consumer issues, resulting in dissatisfied customers and choosing other brands, which eventually led to the startup losing its competitiveness and survival space in the market and bankruptcy.

An e-commerce startup wants to attract customers by selling a lot of lower-priced goods, so that it can earn most of the gross profit. However, this business model, with high operating expenses and poor control of logistics costs, led to heavy debt, default over debt, and eventually led to the startup's bankruptcy.

The competition is brutal

Case:

Xiao Ming is the founder of a newly established small e-commerce company. He spent a lot of time and money to build the company and achieved some success in a short time. However, competitors of the big e-commerce companies began to offer better prices and better services to Xiaoming's customers, and used their size to drive down Xiaoming's profit margins. Xiao Ming's company was badly run and had to go bankrupt.

Xiao Zhang is the founder of an expanding fast-food chain. His brand is very popular in the city and has won a large number of loyal customers. However, his competitors started opening a lot of new stores in the same area and adopted a series of strategies, such as lowering prices and improving service quality. This put great pressure on Xiao Zhang's fast food restaurant, which eventually led to bankruptcy.

Xiao Li is the founder of a startup specializing in land funnel repair and installation services. In the beginning, he successfully started the business and acquired many customers. However, his competitors were too competitive and started offering the same service at a lower price and adopted a more aggressive marketing strategy. This put a lot of financial pressure on Xiao Li's company, which eventually led to bankruptcy.

Low brand value

Case:

Xiao Zhang, a young entrepreneur, opened a sporting goods store, but because the brands he chose were not valuable enough, more people chose to buy sports equipment from big brands, resulting in poor sales of his store. Despite his constant efforts to increase advertising spending and publicity, he eventually went bankrupt due to lack of brand exposure.

Xiao Wang is a young cosmetics entrepreneur who opened a beauty salon, but because her beauty care brand is not valuable enough, more people choose to buy cosmetics from big brands, which makes it difficult for her to gain market share in the market competition. Lacking enough clients, she was eventually forced to shut down her startup.

Xiao Li, a young restaurant entrepreneur, opened a health food store, but because his brand was not valuable enough, more people chose to buy big brands of food, resulting in his store unable to attract enough customers. Despite his attempts to launch new products and promotions, he eventually had to declare bankruptcy due to lack of brand exposure and awareness.

Unstable team

Case:

Xiao Tang and his team members started the business together, and their goal was to develop a smart home device. It went well at first, but after a year, two core members left the company for family reasons, and they left no resources or code behind. Without the contributions of these key people, the company quickly ran into a funding bottleneck and eventually went out of business.

Wang and his team members are working on a social product that aims to provide unified management of users. In the first few months, the team seemed very dynamic, but for a variety of reasons, including disagreements among team members and a lack of working capital, the company quickly ran into trouble. As the team left, clients dwindled and money was lost, they eventually couldn't handle the pressure and went bankrupt.

Ma and her team members co-founded a company that provides online career counseling services. They had the presence of mind to develop state-of-the-art technology solutions, but because the company had no liquid assets to pay its employees, the company's employees disappeared. Later, in order to ensure the digestion of the initial investment, all the assets of the company were hollowed out, but it ended in bankruptcy.

Insufficient investment in marketing

Case:

Miss Su is an entrepreneur who has just founded an environmental brand. Although her product was excellent, her brand didn't get enough exposure in the market because she didn't have enough money for publicity and marketing. Eventually, she went bankrupt and even faced debt recovery.

Mr. Wang has opened a restaurant with a healthy diet, but he hasn't invested enough in advertising and online marketing. As a result, his clientele was too limited to cover the cost of running the restaurant. Eventually, he had to close his restaurant.

Ms. Li started a brand of lipstick made from natural ingredients, but because she didn't have enough publicity and marketing, her brand didn't attract many customers. In order to save costs, she had to choose cheap materials, which eventually led to the decline of the quality of her products and the market reputation was seriously damaged.

Miss Ma invested in a new fruit and vegetable processing plant, but because she did not do enough research and market demand analysis on the market, her products could not meet the needs of customers, especially consumers who are looking for health, natural and low sugar. Soon, her product encountered a bottleneck in the market, and her factory had to lay off a large number of employees and even went bankrupt.

illegal punishment

Case:

Xiao Ming is a young entrepreneur who founded a health food company and sells its products to customers through a mobile app. Soon after, however, his company faced a series of accusations and lawsuits for failing to comply with legal requirements for data protection, resulting in the theft of customers 'private information. Eventually, his company went bankrupt due to huge compensation and fines.

Xiao Zhang is a young man who wants to open his own barbershop. Before he opened the store, he did not notice that the local current regulations have strict requirements for the safety and sanitary conditions of store operations. Due to insufficient fire fighting equipment and fire exits, Xiao Zhang's barber shop was severely damaged in an accidental fire and finally he had to close his business.

Mr. Li, an online marketer, once maliciously tarnished the reputation of a rival company by posting false information on his social media account. Little did he know, however, that such conduct would be considered commercial defamation and illegal. When the case was finally revealed, Xiao Li faced huge compensation and legal proceedings, which eventually led to the bankruptcy of his business.

Xiao Wang was a successful entrepreneur who started a company selling high-end leather goods and quickly gained a dominant position in the market. However, he did not cooperate with government agencies in the process of the company's success and evaded many taxes. When this behavior was exposed, Xiao Wang had to face a high fine, which eventually led to the bankruptcy of his company.

Kobayashi is a young software developer who created a social media platform and made money running it. Because he did not register the company as required by law and did not pay taxes to the tax authorities, Kobayashi's company was deemed to be operating illegally and faced various fines and lawsuits. Eventually, his company had to be shut down and he lost his business and all his investments.

Too much attention to detail

Case:

Xiao Ming, a young entrepreneur who is keen on the catering industry, opened a small restaurant and spent a lot of time and resources decorating the interior environment and polishing the details of the dishes. However, he ignored the analysis of positioning and market demand, which eventually led to the restaurant's inability to attract customers and eventually went bankrupt.

Manager Wang is an entrepreneur who is keen on the clothing industry. He opened a clothing store. He spent a lot of time and money on store decoration and material selection, but he didn't spend too much time and resources on market research, which led to the store's clothing style inconsistent with fashion trends, and eventually faced the same problem.

Mr. Zhang is an entrepreneur who opened a pastry shop. He spent a lot of time and money polishing the raw materials and craftsmanship of the pastry, but he didn't have much time and resources to invest in marketing and customer service, resulting in the pastry shop's brand not being widely publicized, and eventually the customer base was scarce, it was difficult to maintain the business, and eventually it closed down.

Not keeping up with market changes

Case:

John is the founder of a traditional textile company. He was committed to producing high-quality, hand-crafted textiles, but over time there was a growing demand for fast-producing, inexpensive products. John's company couldn't keep up with the trend and was eventually forced into bankruptcy.

Sarah runs a boutique coffee shop that serves very high quality coffee, but is also quite expensive. However, the market is becoming saturated, with customers increasingly preferring to buy cheap instant coffee at convenience stores or large chain cafes. Sarah couldn't compete with these businesses, and eventually the cafe closed down.

Tom, the owner of a small cleaning company, initially attracted some customers with low prices. However, he is reluctant to add new technologies, such as online booking and payments. This allows other companies to provide more convenient services. With the gradual loss of customers, Tom's company couldn't go on and eventually went bankrupt.

Joan is the owner of a family bakery. She is very good at making traditional cakes and cookies. As people became more health-conscious, Joan did not update her products, causing her business to decline. In the absence of timely adaptation to market changes, Joan's store could not continue to operate and eventually went bankrupt.

Jack is the owner of a small family restaurant. His business was good at first, but he didn't adapt to the current trend of consumers preferring takeout and buffet. Under the pressure of competition, he couldn't match his competitors 'prices and service levels. Eventually, Jack's restaurant closed and he lost all his investment.

Partner/investor conflict

Case:

Two partners in a startup are fighting because one wants to expand the company into foreign markets, while the other thinks it's hard enough to grow in the local market. The quarrel eventually led to one party withdrawing, taking away a large amount of investment funds, leaving the company in financial trouble and eventually leading to bankruptcy.

An internet startup receives funding from an investor who forces the company to accelerate its expansion in order to earn a faster return on investment. This has upset the company's founders, who believe the company needs time to fine-tune some issues. The intense pressure from investors led to some wrong decisions, which further worsened the company's financial situation and eventually led to the company's collapse.

A well-known startup attracts capital from multiple investors, but over time, conflicts arise between these investors, mainly because they have different views on the future direction of the company. This led to a shortage of funds and a split in management, which eventually led to bankruptcy.

A husband and wife start a startup and they get the backing of an investor. But then there was a conflict between the husband and wife, which led to a split in the company's management. Among them, one party withdrew from the company and took away a large amount of funds, which made the company fall into financial difficulties and eventually led to bankruptcy.

A start-up is funded by an investment firm, but the management of the investment firm changes and its own people are assigned to the company. This has led to conflicts with the company's management because of the huge differences in the backgrounds and ways of thinking of the two parties.

There was no consensus on the company's strategy and planning, which eventually led to the company's bankruptcy.

Poor quality of product/service

Case:

Xiao Wang, a cake shop owner, bought a very cheap oven to bake cakes when he started his business. However, the oven was of poor quality, not only consumed high power, but also baked cakes that tasted bad, and customers were reluctant to buy them again, eventually leading to the bankruptcy of Xiao Wang's cake shop.

Mr. Liu opened a jewelry store and bought many imported diamonds and gems to sell. However, his suppliers did not provide him with real diamonds and precious stones, but inferior imitations. When customers found that the goods did not meet the description, they began to return the goods, which eventually led to Mr. Liu's store collapse.

Xiao Wu and his partner opened a new car repair shop. They used a very cheap car lift to repair the vehicle, but the lift was of such poor quality that the vehicle accidentally fell during the lift. These accidents damaged many vehicles and damaged the reputation of Xiao Wu's shop, which eventually went bankrupt.

Ms. Xu founded a clothing brand, but the clothes she designed faded and fell off every time she wore them. Because her supplier is to reduce the cost of raw materials to buy inferior materials to make. This made customers very dissatisfied and eventually led to the bankruptcy of Ms. Xu's clothing brand.

Mr. Zhang did a household goods business project. They ordered a batch of exquisite tableware produced in mass production, but these tableware contained harmful substances. When consumers found out, they began to ask for returns and compensation, which led to the rapid decline of Mr. Zhang's household goods brand and eventually went bankrupt.

Entrepreneurs are not persistent enough

Case:

Alice is a young female entrepreneur whose company is an emerging e-commerce platform that aims to break down the barriers between traditional retail stores and brands. However, in the face of difficulties and challenges in the early stage of entrepreneurship, Alice lacked sufficient perseverance and persistence to constantly change the company's strategy and direction. Eventually, the lack of a stable direction and a constantly changing strategy led to declining sales and bankruptcy.

Jack is a young IT entrepreneur whose company focuses on developing smartphone applications. Although his products have been well received in the market, he often ignores the long-term benefits because of immediate benefits. In the face of competitors and changing market demands, he lacked persistence and invested the company's resources in short-term solutions rather than long-term growth strategies. Eventually, this short-sighted decision led to the company's failure and bankruptcy in the fierce market competition.

Sarah is a young social media entrepreneur who started a company called "SocialHub" to provide personalized social media management and marketing services for businesses. Despite her initial excitement, she didn't take into account long-term operating costs and changes in market demand. As she faced business costs and reduced customer demand, she quickly lost patience and motivation and stopped pursuing growth.

Eventually, her company went bankrupt because of a lack of persistence and long-term vision.

disease bankruptcy

own disease

Case:

Mr. Zhang, a young entrepreneur, was diagnosed with severe food allergies shortly after opening a restaurant. Although he tried various methods, such as changing the diet and hiring professionals, the symptoms continued to occur. As the business of the restaurant was badly affected, Mr. Zhang eventually had to close his business and went bankrupt.

Ms. Wu was one of the founders of an innovative medical small business, but in the early days of the company's operations, she suddenly became seriously ill and required a long period of treatment and recovery. Since she was the main organizer and leader of the company, the company ran into trouble and eventually went bankrupt.

Mr. Li is an entrepreneur who has invested in and opened a large-scale amusement park. But later, he was diagnosed with a severe lung disease and doctors ordered surgery. Mr. Li had to close the amusement park and face a series of high medical expenses and loss of income. This led to his eventual bankruptcy.

Disease of relatives

Case:

Xiao Ming's mother has a rare disease that requires expensive treatment, but Xiao Ming's family doesn't have enough savings to pay for it. In order to raise money, Xiao Ming's father had to borrow money and eventually fell into bankruptcy.

After her parents divorced, Xiao Li and her mother lived together. However, when Xiao Li's mother developed cancer, the family's financial situation began to become quite tight. Despite their efforts to cut costs, they still cannot afford expensive medical expenses and daily living expenses, eventually leading to family bankruptcy.

Xiao Wang's family, who lived in the countryside, was originally very privileged, with vast land and many poultry. However, when his father suffered a heart attack and needed expensive surgery, the family had to take out loans. The success rate of the operation was not high, eventually leading to the death of Xiao Wang's father. With the loss of their main breadwinner, Xiao Wang's family could no longer support themselves and went bankrupt.

College student Xiao Ming's family is nearly bankrupt because his father is committed to pursuing a ridiculous business venture that unfortunately ends up causing the family's financial ruin. Xiao Ming's father becomes a loveless financial adventurer in pursuit of his dream, which leads to the collapse of the whole family.

Xiao Zhang's wife suffered a stroke that required expensive treatment and a long recovery period. Because Xiao Zhang's income was not enough to pay for expensive medical expenses, his family had to start selling valuable possessions and even had to borrow money to pay for daily expenses. In the process, Xiao Zhang's family fell into poverty and bankruptcy.

Bankruptcy resulting from a crime

Case:

Mr. Zhang was sentenced to hundreds of thousands of yuan in compensation for illegally stealing other people's property. However, he did not have enough financial resources to bear the compensation and eventually went bankrupt and lost all his property.

Ms. Li was awarded 1 million yuan in compensation for violating her commercial contract, but her business was not prosperous and she could not afford the cost and eventually went bankrupt and closed down.

Mr. Wang was awarded 500,000 yuan in compensation for injuries caused by a traffic accident. However, his job was not very stable and he could not afford the cost and eventually went bankrupt.

Mr. Xu was sentenced for intentional injury and ordered to pay 600,000 yuan in compensation, but he could not get a stable source of income and struggled to repay the debt for several years, eventually losing all his property to bankruptcy.

Stock market, virtual currency and other investment bankruptcy

Case:

Xiao Zhang is a professional investor who has many years of experience in investing in the stock market. He used to make a lot of money in the stock market, but last year he lost a lot of money because of a heavy position in a company's stock, which eventually led to his bankruptcy. This lesson taught him to be cautious about investing.

Xiao Li, a young investor, heard from a friend about how to make money from virtual coins, so he started buying and selling in the market. One of his buying moves resulted in huge losses, he ran out of money and went bankrupt.

Wang is a veteran with a lot of experience investing in the stock market, and he rarely makes mistakes. However, one of his investment decisions last year was unfortunate. He made a lot of investments when he saw the company's stock price skyrocket. However, soon the company's industry encountered a major change, stock prices plummeted, Wang's investment instantly turned into nothing. Eventually, he had to declare bankruptcy.

Divorce, bankruptcy

Case:

Xiaoyu and Xiaoming married less than a year after divorce, Xiaoyu because they do not know how to protect their property, to Xiaoming dragged down their business, and their work has also been affected, and finally went bankrupt.

Mr. Wang spent all his savings within a month because he had to pay alimony and a real estate loan after the divorce. He also paid for his living expenses and his children's tuition, so he went bankrupt.

Ms. Li was mentally depressed after her divorce, unable to concentrate on her work, lost her job, and had to pay a lot of alimony and debt, eventually falling into bankruptcy.

Mr. Zhang's property and vehicles were awarded to his ex-spouse after his divorce because of unfair division of property. He lost important asset support and had to pay alimony and children's education expenses, eventually having to go bankrupt.

go bankrupt after unemployment

Case:

After Mr. Wang lost his job, he had difficulty finding new job opportunities and eventually had to face bankruptcy. As a result, his wife left him, he was unable to maintain his daily life and eventually lost his family and personal dignity.

Ms. Li worked in a company for many years, but she was forced to fire her because of the company's depression. During her brief job search, she was unable to pay her credit cards and home loans, which eventually led to her bankruptcy.

Ms. Wang was injured in a car accident, which left her unable to work for a long time. Her savings were quickly depleted, she couldn't pay her mortgage and medical bills, and eventually had to go bankrupt.

lose a lawsuit and go bankrupt

Case:

Mr. Zhang was sued for violating market regulations during his start-up. Eventually, he lost the case and was awarded hundreds of millions of dollars in compensation. Unable to afford the huge amount of compensation, Mr. Zhang was finally forced to declare bankruptcy and the enterprise closed down.

Ms. Li was sued for wrongful infringement and the case was finally ruled unsuccessful. In order to compensate for the huge compensation, Ms. Li had to mortgage property, cars and other property to pay, eventually leading to personal bankruptcy.

Mr. Wang was fined and criminally prosecuted by the CSRC for insider trading while trading in the stock market. In the end, Mr. Wang lost the case and had to pay a fine of 1 million yuan. Unable to afford it, Mr. Wang had to declare bankruptcy.

Liu was investigated and prosecuted by the Anti-Corruption Bureau for his bribery in construction projects. In the end, Mr. Liu lost the lawsuit and faced decades of prison and huge damages. Unable to afford it, Mr. Liu eventually went bankrupt.

excessive consumption bankruptcy

Case:

Xiao Li is a young white-collar worker who always hopes to bring a better life experience to himself. As a result, his monthly consumption exceeded his actual income. He bought high-end fashion clothes, shoes, cosmetics, etc., and even took out a loan to buy a luxury car. In the end, because he couldn't afford such high consumption, he fell into bankruptcy.

Xiao Zhang is a young entrepreneur whose business has achieved great success in the market. However, he incurred huge debts for personal reasons, especially because of excessive consumption. He often attends private parties and luxury events, and buys all kinds of expensive jewelry, designer watches and cars. When his business began to have some problems, he found himself unable to pay off those debts and eventually went bankrupt.

Xiao Wang is a young student who dreams of a better life. He borrowed a lot of money from usury to pay for his high consumption. He bought all kinds of luxuries, travel, cars and so on. Eventually, when he couldn't repay his high debts, he couldn't avoid bankruptcy.

What are the problems after bankruptcy

credit problem

In China, bad credit refers to the existence of bad information such as overdue repayment, arrears and breach of contract in personal credit records. If the bank debt, it will directly affect the personal credit record, which will have a negative impact on all aspects of the individual.

First of all, bad credit will have an impact on personal credit rating. Because the credit record is taken as an important basis for the bank to judge the personal credit level, once the bad credit record appears after being urged by the bank, the personal credit rating will decline, thus affecting all aspects of personal daily life.

Secondly, bad credit will have an impact on individual loan application. In China, banks must inquire about personal credit records when examining individual loan applications. Once there are bad credit records, they may be refused loan applications or required to provide more collateral, thus increasing the difficulty and cost of applications.

Thirdly, bad credit will have an impact on individual credit card application. In China, applying for a credit card also requires banks to inquire about personal credit records. If an individual's credit record is bad, the success rate of applying for a credit card is greatly reduced, and the application may even be rejected.

Finally, bad credit reporting will affect individual employment and life. In some cases, some companies require employees to provide credit records as a condition of entry. If the individual has bad credit, it may affect the individual's job search and career development.

Case:

Mr. Zhang was unable to repay the bank loan because of bad business and eventually went bankrupt. Because of his bad credit, he could not get credit from other banks, which prevented his business from recovering. In order to make a living, he had to find some usurious loans and eventually fell into a deeper debt crisis.

Ms. Li was unable to repay the bank's mortgage for personal reasons and eventually went bankrupt. Her bad credit has prevented her from getting loans from other banks and has had a lot of trouble even renting a house. Her credit card was withdrawn and she ended up homeless.

Mr. Wang borrowed a sum of money from the bank to do business, but the business suffered a serious loss and was unable to repay the loan and eventually went bankrupt. Because of his bad credit, he could not get loans from other banks or even buy a house. In this case, his marriage also faced great pressure, which eventually led to divorce.

Ms. Zhang invested in some unreliable projects because of her desire for high interest rates, and her debts gradually accumulated, eventually unable to repay the bank's debts and went bankrupt. Because of her bad credit, she could not get loans from other banks, which led to her life in trouble. At the same time, her friends and family began to alienate her, leaving her feeling lonely and helpless.

Mr. Li was eventually sued by the bank and sentenced to bankruptcy because he could not repay his credit card debts. Because of his bad credit, he could not get loans from other banks or rent an ideal house. Even when looking for a job, he suffered some rejection, and eventually he could only live a life close to being homeless.

Legal issues

In China, when the debtor is unable to perform the debt, the creditor can apply to the court for enforcement. The execution procedure needs to go through several stages of trial and judgment, and finally the execution is carried out by the execution court. In the process of execution, some problems may arise for the debtor.

First, the debtor may encounter the problem of property being seized and frozen. In order to protect the interests of the creditor, the enforcement court may first take preservation measures to seal up or freeze the debtor's property to prevent it from selling or transferring the property. This will affect the liquidity of the debtor and affect its normal life and operation.

Second, the debtor may be at risk of being detained. In the execution procedure, if the debtor refuses to perform the executed judgment, the execution court may take compulsory measures such as arrest and detention. These measures may cause a lot of trouble and inconvenience to the debtor.

In addition, debtors may face negative credit records, loss of credit and other problems. In the execution procedure, if the debtor refuses to perform the judgment, the enforcement court may make corresponding records in the personal credit record, which will have adverse effects on the debtor's future life and work.

Finally, the debtor may suffer an additional burden of enforcement costs. In the process of execution, the enforcement court will charge certain fees, including announcement fee, stamp duty, etc., which will be borne by the debtor. In China, debt collection by the court may result in property restrictions, detention and other coercive measures, credit damage, additional costs and other issues.

Case:

Xiao Zhang is an entrepreneur. In order to start his business, he borrowed a sum of money from an investment company. Because the start-up project took a detour, Xiao Zhang was unable to fulfill the repayment promise. The investment company applied to the court for enforcement proceedings. During the execution, the court seized Xiao Zhang's bank account and real estate, which greatly affected Xiao Zhang's life and business. In the end, Xiao Zhang was unable to pay off his debts and was detained for seven days and had to pay high execution fees.

Xiao Li and the company have a contract dispute, and finally the court makes a judgment, requiring Xiao Li to pay certain compensation and liquidated damages. However, Xiao Li has refused to perform the judgment, resulting in the company unable to get due compensation. The enforcement court made corresponding records in Xiao Li's personal credit record, which brought adverse effects to Xiao Li. In the end, Xiao Li was forced to execute the judgment by the court and paid high enforcement fees.

Mr. Wang, the boss of a company, borrowed money from a bank to run the company because of problems in the company's capital chain. But for some reason, Mr. Wang was unable to repay the loan on time. The bank then applied to the court for enforcement procedures and seized Mr. Wang's assets and bank accounts, but he still refused to comply with the judgment. Eventually, the court issued a detention order, and Mr. Wang was detained for several days and paid substantial enforcement fees. The execution also took a huge toll on the company's reputation, with customers leaving and the company in great trouble.

life problem

Many individuals need to liquidate their assets to pay off their debts when they go bankrupt. As a result, individuals need to hand over most of their assets, such as property and vehicles, to the Tribunal for liquidation.

As individuals are required to surrender their assets, the quality of life of families is greatly affected and they may be faced with working hard to meet their living expenses.

In bankruptcy, individuals need to go through legal procedures to clear their debts. As a result, individuals need to follow judicial proceedings, attend court hearings and other formalities to deal with bankruptcy matters. These procedures often require time and effort, placing an additional burden on the individual.

Case:

Xiao Wang was a young entrepreneur who borrowed a large sum of money to start his own company. However, due to the fierce competition in the market, his company kept losing money and eventually went bankrupt. Xiao Wang had to liquidate all his assets to pay off his debts, including his house and cars. He and his family were forced to live in a small apartment, working hard every day to meet basic needs.

Mrs. Su is an old woman who lives alone. All her assets are invested in one company. However, the collapse of the company resulted in the loss of all her investments. As she lives off this investment, she is left with nothing and even has difficulty paying for her daily living expenses. Mrs. Su had to live on government assistance and undergo bankruptcy proceedings in court.

Mr. Zhang is a successful businessman who has made huge profits in many real estate transactions. However, one unfortunate investment led to his bankruptcy. He had to liquidate all his assets to pay his debts. He and his family had to take a back seat and the quality of life plummeted. It has been a very traumatic experience for his family, who have had to say goodbye to looking forward to a bright future and are now struggling to survive.

Mrs. Li, the owner of a small retail store, borrowed a lot of money last year to develop her business. However, due to the fierce competition in the market, her store did not make enough money. She had to liquidate all her assets under pressure from her creditors. Mrs. Lee's life declined sharply and she had to change her lifestyle to cope with the situation. Her days became difficult.

social relation problem

When individuals go bankrupt, their mental and emotional state is also affected. You may feel confused, depressed, and lost, and you may become alienated from your friends and family. Of course, there are many people who will have the support and love of friends and family, but for many, bankruptcy will become a long-term problem in their lives, which will adversely affect their personal relationships. Because in China, many people rely on friends and family loans to build their own business. When individuals go bankrupt, these people will lose their trust, which can have unexpected consequences for their future careers.

Case:

As a young entrepreneur, Xiao Li borrowed money to start a small company. However, due to the market downturn, his company fell into an economic crisis and eventually went bankrupt. Unable to pay off his debts, Xiao Li was forced to close the company, but his debt problem has been bothering him. Due to the influence of negative emotions, Xiao Li and his wife gradually alienated and eventually divorced. Now, Xiao Li is trying to restart his life and career, but his credibility has taken a serious hit and he can no longer get financial support from his circle of friends and relatives.

Xiao Wang is a successful entrepreneur, winning the market with his creative products and making his company realize considerable profits. However, due to the improper operation of his business partner, their company's financial situation plummeted, leading to Xiao Wang's personal bankruptcy. Due to the sudden deterioration of his financial situation, Xiao Wang could not withstand the pressure from banks and creditors, and his relatives and friends could not give him enough support. As a result of his mental illness, Wang often felt depressed and lost, which affected his social and family life.

Xiao Zhang, a young entrepreneur, decided to go to a big city to look for business opportunities. He enlisted the help of friends, borrowed some money from his family and rented a small warehouse. However, due to the market downturn, Xiao Zhang's career suffered a major blow. His warehouse was even more neglected, and he gradually fell into the debt trap and eventually lost his fortune. Due to his debt problems, Xiao Zhang had a rift with many relatives and friends, could no longer get support from them, and finally left his hometown to find new opportunities.

Mental preparation and attitude adjustment

Bankruptcy is an extremely painful thing, it can not only cause significant financial and economic losses, but also have a huge impact on our psychological and social relationships. However, even on the verge of bankruptcy or in the predicament of bankruptcy, we cannot give up, we must be mentally prepared and actively face it.

First, we need to understand that bankruptcy is not failure, nor is it our personal fault or inadequacy. Fluctuations in the current situation, changes in the market, economic instability and other factors may lead to the bankruptcy of enterprises or individuals. So we need to be honest with ourselves and not see our failure as a disgrace, but as an opportunity to accumulate wealth and life experience.

Secondly, we should lay down the psychological burden and not be shrouded by the shadow of bankruptcy. This means that we need to clean up the mental garbage, get rid of negative emotions such as anxiety, worry and self-blame, and find our confidence and courage to actively seek solutions to problems. At the same time, we should look for positive energy information and ideas to fill ourselves with hope and upward motivation.

In addition, we need to adjust our attitude towards family and social relations. When facing family members, we should be honest with each other, inform them as much as possible, share the pressure with family members, and seek solutions together. In the face of society, we should abide by the law, fulfill our debts normally and deal with the relationship with creditors. Moreover, we can also use social resources, receive help and support, actively expand social circles, communicate with experienced people, and improve experience and knowledge.

Finally, we must have faith and perseverance, believe that they will be able to get out of the predicament of bankruptcy. We need to cultivate a strong will and indomitable spirit, continue to learn and improve, and gradually move towards success.

In short, people who are about to go bankrupt or have gone bankrupt need to be mentally prepared, face it calmly, put down their psychological burden, adjust their attitude towards family and social relations, and believe that they will be able to regroup and achieve breakthroughs in their careers and lives.

Case:

Mr. Wang is the boss of a small company, because the market competition intensifies, causes the company's business to shrink gradually. Eventually, the company went bankrupt. Mr. Wang felt very lost, but he did not give up hope and began to look for new opportunities in the business. By actively communicating with the bank and other creditors, he was able to obtain deferrals and remissions on his arrears, which gave him more time to adjust his strategy and reorient the company. Eventually, he found a new market opportunity, successfully revived his company, and achieved great success in business.

Ms. Zhang's family is in financial crisis because of some financial difficulties. She did not give up hope, actively adjusted her mentality and began to look for new job opportunities. She used her Social networks and friends to find a new job, and she confidently demonstrated her abilities and actively adapted to the new work environment. She insists on learning and improving her skills, and has been recognized and trusted by company leaders and colleagues. As a result, her family's finances improved, and her self-confidence and quality of life improved dramatically.

Mr. Li's family business is facing bankruptcy due to poor expansion and mismanagement. In the face of this situation, Mr. Li did not give up, and inspired his entrepreneurial enthusiasm and belief. He actively sought out market opportunities and new partners to help him rebuild his business. He actively communicated with banks and other creditors and played a full coordinating role, eventually obtaining some debt relief and maturity reduction. His hard work in managing his company and focusing on cost control eventually enabled him to overcome the difficulties and regain his competitive edge.

Ms. Wang's family was hit hard financially and forced to sell some of their belongings. However, she did not give up and decided to keep trying to change the outcome. She understood the importance of family financial management and began to look for new job opportunities to increase the family's income. She uses part-time jobs, Taobao stores, offline retail stores and other ways to expand revenue sources. Through their efforts, the family's financial situation has gradually stabilized and finally gradually got rid of financial difficulties.

Mr. Qian's job is facing layoffs, which has left him jobless and in financial trouble. Instead of being discouraged, he looked for new opportunities. He invested a lot of time and energy in further learning new skills, expanding his social circle through Social networks and friends, and learning about new job opportunities. He capitalized on his excellence and eventually found a new job, which enabled him to overcome unemployment and financial difficulties. His motivation and indomitable spirit led him to new successes and a better person.

Chapter 2: Getting Your Finances in Order and Facing Debt

Accounting and analysis of income and expenditure

After a long and difficult period of bankruptcy, there are many people who are struggling to rebuild their finances. However, rebuilding financial stability starts with understanding your income and expenses. The following will introduce how to do the accounting and analysis of income and expenditure, and sort out your financial situation.

The first step is to calculate income

First, list all your sources of income, including salary, rent, investments, etc. After determining your total monthly income, divide it by 30 or 31 to get your average daily income. This is important because it can help you understand how much you can spend each day and thus better control your spending.

The second step is to account for expenses

As with income, list all expenses first, including your child's tuition, rent, utilities, food, transportation, and so on. Make sure you keep track of your monthly expenses and keep a breakdown of what you spend, such as rent as a percentage of your total expenses, food as a percentage of your total expenses, etc. This can help you better evaluate your lifestyle and understand your spending habits.

The third step is analysis

Compare income and expenditure figures to find out which expenses are higher and which can be reduced. If your expenses are higher than your income, then you need to make more efforts to control your expenses. If you spend less, then congratulations, you can save some money to pay off debts.

The final step is to develop a budget

Once you know your monthly income and expenses, you can begin to develop a budget. According to their own living needs and income, develop a reasonable budget to avoid exceeding the scope of expenditure.

Doing an accounting and analysis of your income and expenses can help you better understand your financial situation. If you have already gone through bankruptcy, this is even more important because you need to recover from bankruptcy as quickly as possible. With these steps, you can take better control of your finances and reduce your future financial risks.

Case:

Mr. Li is a small and medium-sized enterprise boss, due to poor management, the company's capital chain problems, eventually led to bankruptcy. Subsequent investigations revealed that he had never conducted a detailed revenue and expenditure analysis and budget planning, so he was unable to adjust his business strategy and led the company into a desperate situation.

Ms. Zhang, a young white-collar worker, bought many designer bags and jewelry, but did not plan her spending, which eventually led to bankruptcy. After realizing her mistake, she began to carefully plan her budget and cut unnecessary expenses in time to reduce financial pressure.

Mr. Wang, a worker, suffered from a serious gambling addiction and often gambled with usury, resulting in a rapid increase in debt and eventual bankruptcy. He regretted it and, after learning about his financial situation, began to actively seek solutions, gradually paying off his debts and starting his life again.

Ms. Yang was a housewife who often worried about household expenses, which eventually led to bankruptcy. She began to carefully account for household expenses, and efforts to find ways to cut spending, and finally effectively control spending, so that family life stabilized.

Mr. Zhang was a young entrepreneur who lacked capital and experience in the early days, which led to poor management of the company and eventually bankruptcy. After gaining a lot of experience, he started his own business again, but he became more cautious, often accounting and analyzing income and expenses, planning budgets, and keeping the company stable.

Types and ranking of debt

When an individual goes bankrupt, they face a wide variety of debts, including credit card debt, consumer loans, mortgages, car loans, taxes, private loan sharks, and so on. So how do we prioritize these different debts?

First, credit card debt is one of the top priorities. Due to the high interest rate of credit card debt, if not repaid in time, it may lead to more and more debt and eventually fall into bankruptcy. As a result, credit card debt needs to be prioritized after personal bankruptcy.

Secondly, if individuals have consumer loans, they also need to be given priority. Consumer loans are usually used to purchase consumer goods such as household appliances and household goods. If they are not repaid in time, interest and fines will be increased, and personal credit records may be adversely affected.

Mortgage and car loans are also types of debt to consider. If an individual has been behind on a mortgage or car payment for several months, the bank will continue to collect and eventually auction off the collateral. Therefore, individuals need to prioritize these debts to avoid further dragging them down. If an individual has a tax deficiency, it also needs to be resolved in a timely manner. Tax authorities have the power to freeze an individual's bank account or even deduct unpaid taxes directly from an individual's payroll account, so individuals need to resolve the tax shortfall as soon as possible.

Finally, consider paying off some of the principal of your private debt. You should try to negotiate the elimination of the interest portion of private debt and the reduction of some principal payments.

In general, post-insolvency resolution of debt issues needs to be categorized according to different circumstances. Only by properly prioritizing debt can individuals be better able to resolve their debt problems and restart their economic journey.

Case:

Mr. Li is an entrepreneur who has achieved success in the wholesale clothing business. However, due to soaring procurement costs and falling market demand, his company fell into bankruptcy crisis. Mr. Li made a positive response, sorted out his own debt types, and through negotiations with the bank, one by one to repay the bank loans owed. Subsequently, Mr. Li also successfully reduced his debt and interest through negotiations with private creditors. He finally managed to get out of the woods and started his own business again.

Ms. Wang is an independent designer working in her own design studio. However, due to the rapidly changing market, her studio was in financial trouble. Ms. Wang knows very well that what she needs to do is sort out her debts and repay the bank loans one by one according to priority. She also actively negotiated with private creditors and successfully reduced her debt and interest payments. In the end, Ms. Wang successfully responded to the crisis and restarted her career.

Mr. Zhang is a young real estate developer. He invested in the construction of a large shopping center, but due to the poor market conditions, his company also fell into bankruptcy. However, Mr. Zhang did not give up. On the contrary, he clearly saw the problems he faced and faced them with a rational attitude. By negotiating with banks and private creditors, he managed to reduce his debt and interest payments. Eventually, Mr. Zhang actively explored new business models and regained success in new markets.

Mr. Huang is the boss of a pharmaceutical company. His company used to be far ahead in the domestic market, but due to new policies and market changes, the company began to fall into bankruptcy crisis. Mr. Huang has shown great composure in the face of difficulties, trying to sort out the types of debts he faces and paying off his debts one by one in order of priority. He also managed to reduce his debt levels by negotiating with banks and private creditors. Finally, Mr. Huang found his foothold in the market again.

Ms. Zheng is a small restaurant owner. Due to the fierce market competition, her small hotel broke the capital chain in a certain period of time and fell into the crisis of bankruptcy. But Ms. Zheng did not give up easily. She sorted out the types of debt she owed and managed to reduce it by negotiating with banks and private creditors. Ms. Zheng eventually readjusted her business strategy and regained success in the market through continuous efforts.

Debt restructuring and repayment plan

realization of assets

Before you restructure your debt, you need to consider selling or discontinuing some of the assets and liabilities that you need to continue to invest cash to maintain. For example: monthly need to repay the loan or spend money on the car, the website subscription members, need to continue to spend money to feed the pet care, regular payment of financial insurance (not recommended to stop the disease and accident insurance), even the balcony You need to spend water every day to water the flowers! Think about what else you need to keep spending money on, sell it or throw it away! These things can't be restructured or repaid, so they need to be sold or thrown away to ease their financial pressure. Although this is painful, believe me, it is necessary.

At present, there are many second-hand markets on the market, such as idle fish, where you can sell useless items (used cars, old furniture, electronics, appliances, etc.) to obtain cash and use it to pay off some of your debts. Although these items sold will not solve all the repayment problems, the money will undoubtedly help you ease the financial pressure and effectively recover the asset value.

Case:

Xiao Wang is the owner of a clothing store, due to fierce market competition, the store did not meet the expected sales, resulting in debt accumulation. In order to repay the debt and improve his finances, Xiao

Wang decided to sell the stock in the store at a low price. Although there will be a certain loss, but can let him get rid of debt trouble.

Mr. Li is a young IT engineer who is constantly buying the latest game consoles and game software due to his love of games. These gaming devices and software kept him spending a lot of money, leading to his poor financial situation. He realized that these gaming devices and software were only assets, but they actually limited his cash flow, so he decided to sell them and use the money to pay off his debts and improve his financial situation.

Xiao Zhang is a salesman. He owns a luxury car. Although the car is his asset, it eats into his cash flow, including gas, insurance, depreciation, and so on. In order to improve his financial situation, Xiao Zhang decided to sell the car and use the money to pay off his debts.

Kobayashi is a pet shop owner. He loves dogs and keeps many pets in his shop. Although these pets seem to be his assets, they are constantly taking up his time and money. In a difficult financial situation, Kobayashi decided to sell the pets and use the money to pay off his debts and improve his financial situation.

Xiao Wang is a real estate developer who has a lot of real estate assets. However, due to poor market conditions, his assets could not be realized in time, which put pressure on his financial situation. In order to improve his financial situation, Xiao Wang decided to sell some of his real estate assets and use the money to pay off his debts. This way, he was able to resolve his financial difficulties and put more money in active markets for more returns.

consolidated debt

Once you have identified which debts need to be paid first, you can start thinking about how to restructure other debts. Debt restructuring is a very complex undertaking and requires an understanding of the various restructuring methods and techniques for negotiating debt restructuring with creditors.

You can choose to combine different debts into one debt to pay off, for example, you can apply for a new loan from a bank to pay off all other debts. The purpose of debt restructuring is to allow you to have better control over your arrears and pay them back more efficiently. But it also means that you need to renegotiate with various creditors, which may not be a smooth process.

Case:

Mr. Zhang is the owner of a small restaurant. Due to market competition, the rise of new stores and poor management of the restaurant, Mr. Zhang's business shrank day by day and finally went bankrupt. He worked on debt restructuring by finding a senior financial adviser. The financial adviser assisted Mr. Zhang in consolidating his debts to the banks and working out a workable repayment plan. Mr. Zhang's subsequent painstaking efforts to repay the loan on time every month have eliminated tensions with creditors.

Ms. Wang started a small furniture manufacturing company. Due to lack of funds, it is necessary to borrow money from several banks. However, due to the high competitive pressure in the market, her business declined and the company went bankrupt. Ms. Wang found a professional debt restructuring company to help her pool her debts and develop a more reasonable repayment plan. In this way, she managed to defuse the tension with the bank and gradually paid off the debt she owed.

Mr. Li's company is at risk of bankruptcy because it is heavily in debt. Mr. Li tried to get the company back on track by constructing a debt restructuring plan, proposing repayment plans to banks and suppliers, and actively looking for new business opportunities. After establishing a new customer base and business channels, Mr. Li successfully repaid all debts and the company also achieved new economic growth.

Ms. Chen is the CEO of a large company. Due to the bad economic situation of the company, she faces huge debts and is threatened with bankruptcy. She found a professional restructuring firm, worked out a workable debt restructuring plan, and presented it to all of the company's creditors. After many negotiations, Ms. Chen successfully resolved the debt crisis, and the company successfully passed the difficulties and returned to the right track.

Ms. Zhang, a real estate developer, has made a lot of money, but she can't cope with market changes, resulting in a shortage of funds for the project. Before she went bankrupt, she found an agency specializing in corporate debt, which helped her successfully restructure the debts of various creditors and develop a repayment plan. In the process of hard work and unremitting repayment, Ms. Zhang gradually paid off her debts to creditors and regained trust and business opportunities.

Specifically, you need to come up with a detailed budget plan to show creditors that you can repay and that the restructuring plan works well. You need to let them know about your willingness to repay and the restoration of your credit in order to get the opportunity to restructure your debt. In this process, you need to pay great attention to business ethics and legal regulations. Only by properly solving the management relationship with creditors can we obtain the best effect of debt restructuring.

transfer of debt

During the debt restructuring process, you may encounter situations such as triangular debt, which refers to debts that are difficult to resolve due to complex relationships between multiple creditors. In this case, you need to resolve the problem through a debt transfer.

A debt transfer is the transfer of debts from multiple creditors to a new creditor. This method allows you to pay only one creditor, thus reducing the management relationship with multiple creditors.

Case:

Mr. Li is a small business owner who went through a bankruptcy in 2022. His company owes more than 2 million yuan, half of which comes from the Bank of China. In order to resolve the debt, Mr. Li decided to transfer part of the debt to other enterprises in order to reduce the risk. He is also actively looking for suitable investors to raise funds through borrowing and equity financing. After two years of hard work, Mr. Li finally got rid of the shadow of bankruptcy, paid off all his debts and ran his own company smoothly.

Ms. Zhang is self-employed and runs a small grocery store. However, Ms. Zhang's store was on the verge of closure in 2021 because of mismanagement and fierce competition. She owed more than $600,000, mostly from several suppliers and a bank. In order to resolve the debt, Ms. Zhang adopted the strategy of debt transfer, lending some financially difficult products to other businesses to obtain funds. At the same time, she is actively looking for other opportunities to cut costs and increase revenue, including reducing expenses, promoting new products, and introducing automation equipment. Now, Ms. Zhang's shop has stood up again, business is getting better and better, and she has successfully paid off all her debts.

Mr. Wang is a young entrepreneur who founded an Internet technology company. However, in 2017, the company's investment failed, resulting in a debt of 1 million yuan. In order to get rid of the debt crisis, Mr. Wang adopted the strategy of debt transfer and cooperated with some other enterprises to transfer part of the debt. He also actively seeks investment opportunities, increases marketing efforts and reduces management costs. After two years of hard work, Mr. Wang's company stood up again and the debt was paid off.

Ms. Li is the founder of a start-up company that successfully explored new markets, but made some mistakes in management that led to debt problems. In order to solve the problem, Ms. Li adopted the strategy of debt transfer, transferring part of the debt to other enterprises and individuals. She also fully communicated with creditors and demonstrated her determination and practical actions to solve the problem. By cutting costs and improving the quality of the company's products, Ms. Li managed to pay off all her debts, get back on her feet and continue to run her business.

Mr. Zhang, a young real estate developer, was involved in a debt crisis in 2020 due to a failed project investment. He owes more than $2 million, half of which comes from the bank. In order to resolve the debt, Mr. Zhang adopted the strategy of debt transfer, transferring part of the debt to other enterprises and individuals, while actively looking for investment and financing opportunities. He has also successfully used his expertise and experience to help other businesses out. By reducing costs, increasing production and sales, and developing new markets, Mr. Zhang's company managed to pay off all its debts within two years and continue to operate.

Chapter 3: Cost of Living Reduction and Optimization

Comprehensive savings in food, clothing, housing and transportation

We should make it clear that we are not passive to save in an all-round way, but active to save in exchange for an early exit from the predicament.

Cut back on food

Eating is something we all have to do, but there are ways we can reduce our food costs. In this case, we need to take some special measures to ensure that we get enough nutrition, while reducing our expenses as much as possible. Here are some dietary tips for the broke.

I only eat what I make at home. The easiest way to economize on food is to cook for yourself. This method is not only the most cost-effective way, but also to ensure that our diet is healthy and hygienic. Don't think that you can't cook, as long as you have the heart, there is nothing impossible.

If you have to eat out, you can bring it from home. If you have to eat out because of work, you can bring it from home. This way you can avoid buying expensive food outside. At the same time, you can bring some fruits and vegetables for yourself, the right amount of nutrients to strengthen their intake, you can also avoid buying snacks outside.

Go to buy more vegetables and other cheap group buying platforms to buy the cheapest vegetables. Many supermarkets or group buying platforms have a variety of fresh vegetables, as long as you pay attention to it, you can buy cheap food. When choosing, be sure to compare the price and quality in order to save more money. You can also learn cooking skills and learn more about gourmet menus so you can eat more delicious, affordable and healthy meals.

Count your food as much as you can to ensure your health. When purchasing food, try to ensure its nutritional value. Choose foods rich in protein, vitamins and minerals. Balance your diet, eat regularly, and eat safely and healthily.

Foods that are easy to preserve can be purchased wholesale as much as possible to save money. When buying food, we not only have to compare prices, but also choose foods that are well preserved and can be stored for a long time. If we can buy with family or colleagues, we can enjoy more discounts. These foods can be stored in the refrigerator and stored at one time, reducing the number of purchases per purchase and saving money.

Cancel all snacks. Snacks are an integral part of our day, but not only are they unhealthy choices, they can cause us to gain weight and waste our money. Minimize or eliminate all snacks, choose healthy foods, and drink water instead of snacks is also a good choice.

In short, saving money on food requires us to do some homework when buying and choose more affordable foods. But despite limited funding, we cannot sacrifice our health and nutrition. Therefore, calculate the nutrition of food as much as possible and make a balanced diet plan. As long as we have the heart, we will certainly be able to achieve better savings in eating.

Case:

Mr. Zhang, the owner of a small restaurant, went bankrupt as a result of the epidemic. However, Mr. Zhang did not give up, he returned home, learned to cook all kinds of food by himself, and never went to restaurants to eat again. After a long period of healthy eating, he regained his physical strength and mental health, and eventually regrouped and reopened a restaurant.

Xiao Lin is a young white-collar worker who is often tired and malnourished due to work pressure. Then he realized his lifestyle needed to change, so he started cooking his own food to ensure the health and quality of the food. Despite the time and effort he spent at the beginning, he soon found that his nutrition and health improved as he no longer relied on takeout and fast food.

Ms. Li, an unemployed single mother, had to change her lifestyle and learn to cook for herself because she had no income after losing her job. She buys basic ingredients from the supermarket, cooks her own meals and no longer spends most of her income eating out. After a few months, she realized that her purse was less tight, and she found herself more confident and courageous than before.

Mr. Wang was an executive who lost his job because the company was not doing well. Despite his low self-esteem, he didn't give up, lose or escape reality, but began a new adventure-cooking for himself. Preparing nutritious food at home made him a "life-loving" person again. After rethinking and adjusting his lifestyle, he finally overcame all difficulties and found his place again.

Miss Zhao is a direct seller, due to the impact of the epidemic, she faced enormous economic pressure, customer loss is serious, performance decline. In order to make a living, she had to start cooking for herself. Although the process required more time and effort in the beginning, she found herself enjoying the cooking process and practicing her cooking skills. Over time, clients slowly came back and she was out of financial trouble.

Cut back on living expenses

Bankruptcy is a heavy topic. In life, clothing is one of our unavoidable expenses, but how to save money on clothing is a problem we need to think about. Here, I'm going to give you a few tips on how to save money on clothes for the bankrupt, and I hope it will help you a little.

First, as long as you are not naked, you must not buy new clothes. Sometimes we are seduced by the lure of fashion and always want new clothes to maintain our image. But the truth is, we often have a lot of clothes in our closets that are used but hardly used. Why not try to create more combinations with the clothes you already have? Cutting back on unnecessary purchases will not only save you money, but it will also be environmentally friendly.

Second, wear as many work clothes as possible. If you have a job that requires you to wear a uniform, you are in luck. You can wear work clothes as much as possible, which not only protects ordinary clothes, but also reduces other expenses, such as the need to buy special cold equipment.

Third, first meet the needs of children, they will become smaller as the body develops. Bankruptcy families with young children at home must first meet the needs of their children. As children's bodies are developing, their clothes quickly become unsuitable. Therefore, we can find some good quality and cheap children's clothes in the online store or second-hand market, so we can save a sum of money.

Fourth, don't be afraid to have no self-esteem, boldly ask for and accept donations from relatives and friends. Sometimes we have to face the unexpected circumstances of life. At this time, we can boldly seek help from relatives and friends. They may have some used clothes that they can give us. While it may sometimes require us to swallow a bit of our pride, doing so can help us in difficult times.

In short, clothing is an essential part of our lives and part of our daily expenses. But there are a few simple tricks we can do to save as much money as possible. I hope these tips can help the needy bankrupts, and I hope you don't give up easily and try to face the difficulties of life.

Case:

Xiao Zhang, the owner of a restaurant, eventually went bankrupt because of poor business affected by the epidemic. However, Xiao Zhang did not give up on this. He began to scrimp and save, put on his work clothes and stopped buying new clothes. At the same time, he also actively asked relatives and friends for old clothes to save money. After a period of hard work, Xiao Zhang restarted his business and achieved new success.

Mr. Liu is a middle-aged man who was once an executive in a successful business. For some reason, he eventually lost his job. In order to save money, Mr. Liu began to wear work clothes and refused to buy new clothes. Although he suffered setbacks and disappointments in his career, his tenacity and courage allowed him to successfully get rid of difficulties and find a better job again.

Kobayashi is a young mother who is unable to work due to a congenital disability. To support her family, she began wearing work clothes and accepting donations of old clothes from relatives and friends. She worked hard to scrimp and save and eventually succeeded in starting a small business and became a well-known figure in the community.

Mr. Wang was an employee of a courier company, and his company eventually went bankrupt because of fierce competition in the industry. To save money, Mr. Wang began to wear work clothes and accept old clothes from relatives and friends. He tried to find new job opportunities and got a better job in a new company. He thought it was just a haze in front of him and a better future awaited him.

Miss Li is a young actress. Her job is not stable because she has been in the industry for a short time. To support herself, she began to wear work clothes and cut down on new clothes as much as possible. After a period of hard work, she successfully signed a new contract and grew into a popular actress. Her proud experience of wearing overalls was widely praised.

Cut back on living expenses

Bankruptcy is a very serious problem for anyone, because in addition to debt, many people will lose their homes. In this case, saving money is crucial for the bankrupt, as they need to cut expenses as much as possible to pay what they owe. Here are some tips to help the bankrupt save as much money as possible when finding a place to live.

Sell the house

If the bankrupt is making expensive monthly mortgage payments, selling the house is a good option. This would ease the burden on the bankrupt and provide them with more money to pay their debts. If bankrupts need a secure place to live, they can consider renting to provide more flexibility for future financial difficulties.

negotiated rent

If the bankrupt is renting, they can negotiate with the landlord to reduce the rent. For landlords, they want to keep stable tenants for a long time, while for bankrupts, reducing rent can help them save more money.

Find a place with a low cost of living

Bankruptcies can choose to move to a low-cost place to live, which can reduce living expenses. For example, they could choose to move to a city with lower rents, or move to an area farther from their workplace but with lower prices.

Ask the boss for help

If the bankrupt's boss is very understanding of their situation, then they can talk to the boss about whether to provide accommodation, which can help them save money.

Camping in parks, rotten houses or bridge holes

If the bankrupt really can't pay the rent, they can choose to go to the park, the unfinished housing community or the bridge hole camping to tide over the difficulties. It's not an ideal option, but at least it can help them get through it. It is important to note that the campsite must be safe and not go to an unsafe place to camp. Try to find a place close to the toilet, as this will make it easier for you to get water and live. You can open a hotel room every 1 or 2 weeks and take a shower to clean up. During this period, I kept telling myself that I was not a homeless tramp, I was just out camping, and I would soon be out of trouble.

All in all, bankruptcy is a very difficult time for anyone, but by taking the above measures, the bankrupt can reduce their living expenses and save as much money as possible to pay the arrears. When things get better, they can move to a better place to live.

Case:

Xiao Wang, a young man who had just gone bankrupt, cut his expenses by selling his property and renting a low-cost apartment. In addition, he started walking to work every day, reducing transportation costs and making a positive change for his finances.

Mr. Li, an employee of a small company, had his salary cut in half because of the company's financial problems. He greatly reduced his expenses by renting the dormitory provided by the company, and spent all the money saved every month to pay off his debts. After several months, he finally managed to get out of trouble.

Lao Zhang, a retired man of about 80, was forced to camp in a park because of his family's financial difficulties. Although life is very simple, he often shares his experiences and stories with other campers, gets a lot of support and help, and his mood becomes very positive. After a period of hard work, he succeeded in getting out of bankruptcy.

Mr. Wang was a businessman who had failed in his business. He had to stay at a friend's house because he had nothing left after bankruptcy. Influenced by his friends, he began to try to save money, eating only simple meals every day, not buying luxury goods, half a year later, he got rid of debt, regained confidence, and began his own road to entrepreneurship.

Xiao Li, an office worker who went bankrupt because of personal debt problems, began moving to a cheap house in the outer suburbs of the city. Although the living conditions are relatively simple, he still gets up early every day to catch up with work time. He kept working hard, looking for new opportunities, and after a few months, he managed to find a stable job and get out of the financial mess.

Cut back on living expenses

For people who are broke, transportation is a problem they have to face. In daily life, the cost of travel usually accounts for a considerable proportion of a person's consumption. In order to be able to save as much as possible on transportation costs, the bankrupt should take the following measures:

Borrow a car for the road. Borrowing a bicycle from a relative or friend that they don't use for the time being is a very economical way to reduce travel costs.

Choose the second-hand car market. If you can't borrow a bike, go to a second-hand market and buy a cheap one. Although it is not as good as a new car, it can meet the travel needs and the price is more affordable.

Reduce taxi travel. Unless you need to go to the hospital for emergency treatment, the bankrupt should avoid taxis as much as possible and choose more economical ways to travel.

Choose public transportation. As the main mode of transportation in cities, buses are more affordable than other modes of transportation, and they can reduce traffic congestion and are more environmentally friendly.

Be careful not to drive illegally. If you really have to keep your car and can't choose other modes of travel, then be careful not to be fined for violations anyway, so as to avoid additional transportation costs due to fines.

Carpool with colleagues whenever possible. If you work far away, you can carpool with colleagues, which can reduce the use of cars and help improve travel efficiency and reduce travel costs.

In a word, the bankrupt should actively take various economical measures to save the travel cost as much as possible, so as to get some help and support economically.

Case:

Mr. Li is the boss of a small company, because the business was affected by the epidemic, the company mismanaged, resulting in a broken capital chain, eventually bankruptcy. After going bankrupt, Mr. Li began to save money in various ways, such as buying second-hand bicycles, riding bicycles instead of driving, avoiding taxis, choosing public transportation and sharing with colleagues. These methods effectively eased his life pressure and gradually helped him get out of trouble.

Ms. Zhang is a novice investor. She made a mistake in the stock market that caused her to lose a lot of money and even went bankrupt. After going bankrupt, Ms. Zhang realized that she needed to control her expenses, so she began to cut down on eating out, cooking by herself, shopping less, buying only what she really needed, and renting a house with friends to reduce housing expenses. These frugality measures helped her gradually out of bankruptcy.

Mr. Wang, a freelancer with a volatile income stream, has faced financial problems and even the threat of bankruptcy as business has fallen short of expectations in recent months. Mr. Wang began to save money by buying defective or second-hand office equipment, avoiding eating out as much as possible, choosing to buy food ingredients online, and controlling living expenses and planning a monthly budget. These measures effectively reduced his financial pressure and helped him gradually out of bankruptcy.

Ms. Huang worked as a waitress in a small restaurant. Due to the impact of the epidemic, the business of the restaurant began to become slow, eventually leading to the loss of Ms. Huang's job. Ms. Huang began to feel financial difficulties after losing her job, but she didn't give up. Instead, she began to actively look for a job and began to take some money-saving measures, such as riding a bicycle instead of taking a taxi, reducing shopping expenses, and saving daily necessities as much as possible. Finally, she found a better job and perked up.

Mr. Xu is a student studying in other places. Due to the pressure of tuition and living expenses, he began to overdraw his credit card gradually and eventually faced the risk of debt bankruptcy. Mr. Xu began to plan and control the funds. He gradually paid off his credit card debts and gradually got rid of the dilemma of debt bankruptcy by reducing his activities, limiting his consumption and sharing a house with his classmates.

After retirement, Ms. Yang began to enjoy her wealth over the years, buying expensive cars, traveling to Europe and America, etc. But as she grew older, Ms. Yang began to have health problems, as well as her financial situation. Ms. Yang began to realize that she needed to control her financial expenses. She decided to start using public transportation to reduce her gas bill, choose healthy foods, and plan her life carefully. These money-saving and planning measures allowed her to adjust to retirement and get out of financial trouble.

Choice and purchase of necessities

For a bankrupt, buying the necessities of life can be a very difficult task. In this process, every penny needs to be carefully considered to make the best use of limited financial resources. Here are some tips to guide the bankrupt on how to choose to buy necessities.

Looking for cheap alternatives

Do everything you can to save money and reduce unnecessary expenses. When buying necessities of life, try to choose cheaper and more practical goods. For example, 2 yuan of soap can achieve the purpose of cleaning the body, there is no need to spend 20 yuan to buy shower gel. In addition, it is also necessary to find all the cheap goods that can be replaced.

Case:

After his bankruptcy, Mr. Chen cut his monthly expenses by a third by finding inexpensive office equipment and supplies. He used the money he saved to invest in a small company and, within two years, grew it into a start-up technology company.

When her baby was born, Ms. Wang suddenly lost her job. She started looking for inexpensive medical supplies and baby products, saving half of her monthly expenses. Her frugality allowed her to have enough money to open a kindergarten at home.

Mr. Lin lost his company, but he didn't want to give up his business spirit. He looked for alternatives to cut costs and opened a small bakery. By saving money and focusing on training and quality improvement, he expanded his bakery into a chain.

Ms. Qian's company had a serious financial crisis, forcing the company to go bankrupt. In this difficult situation, Ms. Qian began to look online for affordable housing and daily control, saving more than half of her monthly expenses. She used the money she saved to start a logistics company and quickly became a market leader.

Mr. Sun went bankrupt because of medical expenses and began to look for cheap drugs and medical equipment to alleviate his illness. He patiently searched and compared, saving more than one million yuan in two years. With this savings, he began to expand his small business, starting a medical device company. It no longer needs to rely on imported equipment from abroad, and it is becoming more and more competitive in the market.

Squeeze more money into education

Use the money saved to buy books, courses, etc. After bankruptcy, better prepare for the future and enhance your knowledge and ability. Therefore, we need to invest more in knowledge learning and improve our competitiveness.

Case:

Xiao Zhang is a young man who has just gone bankrupt. He has lost his job and is burdened with huge debts. He didn't give up, and he started to save money by buying books and watching online courses. Through his studies, he acquired new knowledge and skills, and he succeeded in finding a better job, getting out of debt, and getting a new lease on life.

Xiao Li is an unemployed woman who lives in poverty with her young children. On the advice of a friend, she enrolled in a technology course online and learned new skills through distance learning. She decided to open a small shop and sell things through her craft to earn money to get out of financial trouble.

Kobayashi lost his job due to an accident, and he was stuck in a loop, unable to find a better job. He began practicing online classes every day, reading educational books and learning new skills. A few months later, he was invited for an interview for a high-paying job and successfully landed it. Through his studies, he became a more valuable employee and also started his life anew.

Xiao Wang's family life has not been easy. His father is ill and has no insurance or savings to pay for medical expenses. Wang didn't give up. He decided to earn extra income to pay for medical expenses by learning online courses and market sales skills. Through his efforts, he succeeded in mastering new skills, he earned more money, and successfully paid for his father's medical expenses.

Xiao Huang is a college graduate who has trouble finding a job. He began using the savings to take online courses and read educational books. He finally mastered his new skills and succeeded in getting a job in a company. Through his efforts, he became the best in the industry and also gained a better life.

Think of yourself as an ancient man

Think of yourself as an ancient person and stay as far away from the supermarket as possible. The supermarket is full of goods, it is easy to lose control, waste their already tight financial resources. Therefore, don't give yourself the opportunity to go to the supermarket and control yourself to buy only necessities.

Case:

Mr. Wang is an ordinary office worker with a meager income and a heavy burden of living. He had been saddled with huge debts because of irrational spending habits and couldn't turn over. However, he decided to strictly control his desire to spend, stop buying unnecessary items and avoid going to the supermarket, saving all the money he could save every month. After several years of persistence, he finally saved a sum of money, paid off all his debts, and used the remaining funds to buy his dream house. Today, he and his family live a happy and stable life.

Ms. Zhang is a single mother who has fallen into deep debt because of family reasons. After a long and difficult time, she finally realized her bad spending habits and began to control her spending and reduce unnecessary expenses. At the same time, she began to study all kinds of financial knowledge on her own to earn more income to pay off her debts. After constant efforts, she finally succeeded in getting out of the debt quagmire and achieved financial independence and autonomy.

Mr. Li is a middle-aged man who lost his job and financial resources due to a series of unfortunate events and had to borrow money from the bank to cover the expenses of his family and the tuition fees of his children. However, due to his lack of financial knowledge, he soon became addicted to excessive consumption and usury, and eventually took on huge debts. In order to change this situation, he began to save money at home, avoid unnecessary expenses, and began to read a variety of books on financial management, while studying and working hard, he successfully paid off all debts.

Ms. Zhu is a young mother who is in a difficult situation, including financial difficulties, because of family changes. However, she did not give up, but riveted her strength forward. She began to master all kinds of knowledge about financial management and investment, successfully paid off all her debts, and learned how to make the right decisions for her future and the happiness of her family.

Mr. Zhao was an ambitious young man. After his first investment failure, he carefully examined his spending habits, began to exercise self-discipline, cut unnecessary expenses, and gradually saved a sum of money to reserve enough funds for his business plan. He started his career in the field he loved and made remarkable achievements. In the process, he also learned to constantly improve his financial knowledge to adapt to changing market conditions.

Prepare the escape pack

If you feel that the creditor is very fierce and may hurt you, you need to prepare a backpack for escape in advance, including some necessary daily necessities, important documents, cash, etc.

Case:

Xiao Zhang, a young waiter, was forced to borrow some usury money because his family was poor and he couldn't pay his father's high medical bills due to illness. With his meagre income, he was unable to pay his debts on time, so his creditors began to threaten him with various means. Xiao Zhang knew he had to take action to solve the problem, so he quit his job as a waiter and fled to another city. There, he found a better job that allowed him to gradually pay off his debts and eventually become a successful entrepreneur.

Xiao Li is a recent college graduate who borrowed money from a bank when he was a student. But because his major was not popular, he found it difficult to find an ideal job after graduation. When he failed to pay his debts on time, his creditors became increasingly aggressive, scaring Xiao Li. To solve this problem, Xiao Li decided to give up looking for a job in the city and choose to go to a remote rural area instead. There, he helped the local people grow vegetables and worked hard every day. His tenacity and perseverance paid off, and within a few years, he paid off all his debts and started his own agricultural company.

Xiao Wang is a young shopkeeper. While he was running his new store,

Xiao Wang met some bad creditors who kept pressuring him to pay his debts. The threats and constant intimidation made Wang feel very depressed. He felt no hope in life. So he decided to run away, he picked up his luggage, went to a strange city, and finally found a well-paid job. Although he has left his shop, he has not given up his enthusiasm. Eventually, he rebuilt his business in the new city and got back on his feet.

Xiao Liu is a young laborer, his living expenses are tight, so he once borrowed some usury from some illegal creditors. When he couldn't pay, the creditors began to increase their threats through home visits. Xiao Liu knew he couldn't live in such an environment. So he bought some light travel bags, packed up everything, and left the city to look for opportunities in another city. There, he found a stable job and started a new life. A few years later, Xiao Liu paid off all his debts and opened his own machinery factory.

Xiao Chen, a young accountant living in poverty, could not pay the high medical bills his mother owed because of her illness, so he borrowed money from illegal lending companies. But when he failed to make his payments on time, the companies began resorting to threats and violence. Chen decided that rather than making his family pay for historical debts, he would rather flee the place. He left his hometown and went to other places to look for a job. In a new city, he found a good job and began to live a new life. Gradually, he overcame his fear of debt and started his own finance company, becoming his own boss.

Never get pregnant

Finally, no matter how poor, contraceptives such as condoms should be purchased. Because the bankrupt couldn't afford to get pregnant. If you're a woman, you need to be aware of this. If you are a man, then please for the family debt, do not let his wife pregnant.

Case:

Xiao Li is a young man who has just lost his job. He comes from a poor family. His parents died and he became the pillar of the family. However, the unexpected pregnancy of his wife made their lives more difficult, and the couple had to spend a lot of medical expenses on treatment. Because Xiao Li has lost his job, the family's expenses were once unbearable, eventually borrowing accumulated, deep in debt quagmire.

Xiao Zhang is a single mother who lives in poverty and raises young children while working. After she became pregnant, doctors told her she needed to stay in bed, which prevented her from continuing to work and earn an income. At this time, the cost of supporting children becomes higher and higher, and medical expenses are also a big expense. Without sufficient financial resources, she could only keep borrowing and eventually could not pay off her debts.

An elderly couple living in a poor mountain village, they are retired workers but have conscience. When they learned that a young woman nearby had been abandoned by her boyfriend after becoming pregnant and could not afford childbirth and medical expenses, the couple did not hesitate to contribute to the rescue. They borrowed a lot of money for this, but in the end they couldn't pay it back and fell into debt.

Xiao Wang is a young migrant worker who came to the city to work because of poverty. Without extra money, he still has to meet the upcoming baby. But the process did not go well, and his wife suffered from a serious illness due to pregnancy and needed expensive medical support. Afraid to ask his parents and friends for financial help, he ended up borrowing money to run his family and was mired in debt.

These are some of the key points that guide the bankrupt to consider when purchasing necessities. In short, in order to use financial resources effectively, precise decisions must be made for every penny. Only in this way can we get out of the predicament faster and lay a better foundation for the future.

Strategies and techniques for saving

As a bankrupt, how to better save financial resources is a very critical and urgent issue. People often fall into despair and anxiety in the face of difficulties, but the right methods and strategies can help you regain control of your finances. In this article, I will provide some guidance and advice on two aspects: establishing a budget mechanism and reducing debt.

Budget mechanism established and implemented

First of all, I would like to emphasize the establishment of budgetary mechanisms. Budget mechanism is a very basic concept, but it is seldom paid attention to and implemented in practice. A clear budget plan can help you get a better handle on your finances and avoid making unnecessary spending and decisions when you're in trouble. First, you need to set a fixed budget that you can afford. Within this amount, you need to consider your living expenses and necessary expenses, which are priorities. However, in order to deal with possible emergencies, you also need to set aside some contingency reserves. This money can be used for unexpected expenses or emergencies, such as sudden medical expenses or family emergencies.

Case:

Xiao Wang's family lives in a small city. His parents often worry about not being able to pay off their debts. By chance, Xiao Wang learned the importance of family budget and immediately discussed with his parents to set up a clear budget mechanism. By resolutely implementing and recording every expenditure in the book, the Wang family successfully got rid of the debt quagmire and began to painstakingly and happily store the income and expenditure of the family economy.

Uncle Wang was in debt and unable to pay his debts because of the failure of his business. However, after meeting financial experts, he began to develop a clear family budget and carried out various specific measures to reduce expenses. Eventually, he succeeded in reducing the size of debt and mastering the financial control of the family. Based on this, he started a new industry.

The Chens have been living in poverty because they can't plan their household expenses properly. By chance, they met an experienced financial expert. Experts help them to develop family budgets, but also provide a variety of financial knowledge about saving, rational consumption and so on. As a result, the family got rid of the long-term lack of food and clothing, and the standard of living gradually improved.

Mr. Zhang's family business has suffered huge losses and is at risk of debt. By chance, after they attended a professional training on family budget and financial management, Mr. Zhang immediately implemented the family strategy and resolutely implemented it. He succeeded in reducing household expenses and gradually paid off his debts, laying a solid foundation for the revival of his business.

Because of the low income of working, Ms. Wang can not afford to buy her own house, even rent a house money is laborious. After learning the basics of family financial management, she began prioritizing and optimizing her plans, earning a small income to make buying a home a reality. Ms. Wang's example has also positively encouraged many families to work together to form a plan, which has greatly improved their quality of life.

Reduce debt and maintain cash flow

Second, we need to think about how to reduce debt. In tough times, reducing debt is critical because it's the only way to get your finances back on track. To reduce debt, we need to take a hard look at our finances and determine what will increase our debt burden and what can be optimized and reduced. In practice, we should reduce expenses and outlays as much as possible, and try not to borrow or fall into a deeper debt trap. In addition, when dealing with assets, we should pay attention to seize market opportunities, buy or sell in time, and obtain positive returns as much as possible. For example, we usually think of our homes and cars as assets, but if they require us to keep pouring cash into them, or if they are driving us deeper into debt, then they are liabilities to us and we need to sell or get rid of them. Once we've reduced our debt, we need to go back to the first step, refocus our budget and better plan our financial path forward.

Case:

Mr. Li, a white-collar worker in Beijing City, once bought a relatively large but poorly located house, but the interest on the loan made him unable to pay the monthly mortgage. In order to avoid being urged by the bank, Mr. Li successfully obtained an income by selling the house. He used the money to buy a smaller apartment in a better location, and then improved his finances by renting it out, reducing debt and generating significant positive cash flow.

Ms. Wang and her husband, a middle-aged couple, once bought a house in downtown Nanjing City, but they couldn't afford the monthly repayment because her husband was unemployed and the interest on the loan was too high. They considered renting out their house to help pay off their debts, but found the rent was too low. Eventually, they decided to sell the house and buy a mini-apartment at the subway entrance for a lower price but in a better location. They rented out their apartment and quickly gained a positive cash flow, not only paying off their debts but also making more money every month.

Mr. Zhang, a young IT engineer, bought a three-bedroom suburbs home on a bank loan. However, due to his remote location, the house he bought was idle and could not be rented, and the interest on the loan gradually accumulated, making him almost unbearable. Mr. Zhang decided to sell the house and use the money to buy a smaller apartment, but in a better location, for rent. The decision took an initial toll, but after a few years of leasing, he managed to reduce his debt and began to work his way out of it.

Xiao Liu, a young professional woman, was once unable to afford a high mortgage from a bank loan to buy a shop. She started thinking about selling the store to reduce her debt, but found it hard to sell. Eventually, she decided to sell cheaply and use the money to buy a small apartment in a better location for rent. The decision almost saved her from bankruptcy and greatly improved her financial situation.

Mr. Chen is a retired worker who once bought a bigger house with a bank loan. His wife had died, leaving him and his son alone, but the interest on the loan was driving him into bankruptcy. He decided to sell the house and use the money to buy a smaller, more secluded apartment. Although the decision cost him a lot of space, he managed to avoid debt. His financial situation gradually improved and he managed to get out of debt.

In a word, as a bankrupt, how to save financial resources is a very urgent problem, but the right methods and strategies can help us regain control of our financial situation. In practice, we should establish a budget mechanism, make a clear budget plan, and set aside contingency reserves. At the same time, we need to reduce debt, optimize expenses, and sell or get rid of unprofitable assets in a timely manner. These positive actions will help us re-establish our financial footing and better prepare us for the difficult economic times we face.

The money-saving artifact of the online world

In today's society, the economic situation is unstable, and more and more people are caught in economic difficulties. And there are many money-saving artifacts in the online world that can help bankrupt people save money. Here are some common ways to save money and help bankrupts make better use of the resources of the online world.

Price comparison shopping plug-in

When shopping online, the price of the same product can vary widely between sellers with different prices. Using the comparison shopping plugin, you can help the bankrupt quickly find the lowest price of the goods, thus avoiding spending too much money.

The Edge browser's price comparison shopping plug-in "Shopping Party Automatic Price Comparison Tool" is a very convenient tool. The installation method is very simple, just visit the extension app store in the

Edge browser, search and install the "shopping party automatic price comparison tool" plug-in. When you look at items on Taobao, Jingdong and other shopping sites, it can automatically show the prices of other sellers and help you find the lowest price on the whole network.

Case:

Mr. Li, an unemployed man, began learning how to use the Internet to help him save money because his family was struggling financially. He learned that the shopping party automatic price comparison tool plug-in can compare the prices of major e-commerce platforms and find the best deals. He bought household necessities online and saved 50% of his expenses after using the plug-in of the shopping party automatic price comparison tool, which helped him through difficult times.

Ms. Liu is an elderly person living alone and her economic conditions are worrying. Unable to shop at the market, she began learning how to use the Internet to shop. Through the shopping party automatic price comparison tool plug-in, she successfully found cheaper than the supermarket goods, saving a lot of money. The use of the shopping party automatic price comparison tool plug-in has helped her through the difficult days both materially and spiritually.

Mr. Zhang is a bankrupt entrepreneur who lost everything in the economic crisis and was forced to become a handyman. Through the plug-in of the shopping party automatic price comparison tool, he successfully saved a lot of expenses. He learned from his entrepreneurial experience and found another opportunity to become a small trader.

Ms. Yang is a single woman who often faces financial difficulties. She learned to use the shopping party automatic price comparison tool plug-in and bought necessities cheaper than supermarkets. She saved money while improving her quality of life, buying quality goods and getting through tough times.

Mr. Feng is a village teacher, living in poverty. He heard that using professional browser extensions can compare prices across major e-commerce platforms and find the best deals. He learned how to use the shopping party automatic price comparison tool plug-in, successfully saved some expenses. The use of the plug-in of the shopping party automatic price comparison tool not only helped him improve his life, but also taught him to make better use of online resources in his daily life.

Use a lot of treasures to get rebates

Duoduo Jinbao is an open platform for Dianduo, providing users with a platform for shopping rebate, and users can get commission rebate by promoting commodities. Bankruptcies can save some of their expenses by enjoying rebates on purchases through the software. Easy to use, just download and register Duoduo Jinbao, you can enjoy rebate discount.

Case:

Mr. Zhang, an expatriate who immigrated to China, has had to struggle on the brink of bankruptcy due to the high cost of living and economic pressures. Fortunately, the small advertisement on his desk led him to discover Duoduo Jinbao, a discount shopping platform. By using the platform to purchase various goods, Mr. Zhang succeeded in being able to afford the cost of living he needed, and earned additional commissions by reintroducing Pinduoduo goods. These commissions allowed him to ease the financial pressure and eventually get out of debt.

Ms. Wang is a single mother who often worries that she can't take care of her children because of the financial burden. After all her attempts to borrow money failed, she began looking for other ways to relieve her stress. Soon, she found a lot of treasures. By buying goods on the platform and recommending others to buy them, Wang not only received preferential hospitality, but also earned a lot of commissions. This extra income allowed her to financially support her children and get out of debt.

Mr LI is an unemployed worker who has been looking for a job for a long time but has not been able to find a job. He was deeply in debt because he feared he would not be able to pay his rent and other living expenses. However, at the suggestion of a friend, he began to use Duoduo Jinbao to buy goods. While shopping, he also successfully contributed to the sales volume of more goods, so he received a commission. By constantly selling more goods, he finally had enough commissions to get out of the debt trap by paying off his debts.

Ms. Zhang is a well-off leftover woman who keeps up with the Joneses because of her lack of self-recognition, leading to rising debt. Frightened,

Ms. Zhang began to take a hard look at her personal life and try to find a better financial solution. Soon, she heard about Duoduo Jinbao, a discount shopping platform. By shopping and promoting on the platform, she earned a lot of commissions, successfully got out of debt, and realized that personal self-worth is more important.

Mr. Ji is an investment failure, bankruptcy of the rich businessman, he can not see hope, life was facing collapse. But Mr. Ji did not give up and began to look for other feasible solutions. More treasure gave him hope, he began to buy two-insurance products, at the same time to introduce more goods to get more commission. Increasingly, these commissions became the key to getting out of debt. Through perseverance and the effective use of tools other than buying and selling, he eventually got out of the mire.

Use what's worth buying to find the lowest price

What is worth buying is a price comparison search engine that can find the lowest price of goods online, better for users to save money. When shopping, users simply search for the desired product and list the lowest price sellers currently on the market. As long as you buy at the lowest price, you can spend as little as possible. At the same time, what is worth buying also provides free trial activities, users can apply for free trial products, not only save money, but also get the evaluation of physical goods.

Case:

Mr. Li's mismanagement led to the bankruptcy of his company, and his days became particularly tight. He bought a mobile phone through a website worth buying, which was cheaper than any one on the market and saved a lot of money. Because of his reliance on the site, he is also posting a blog called "How to Save Money in Bankruptcy." This blog has received a lot of attention, and he has received a lot of appreciation and thanks for the comments, which has brought him some warmth and hope.

Ms. Wang likes cosmetics very much, but her salary is not high, so she saves a lot of money every month. She found a great deal on a website worth buying, so she decisively placed an order for her favorite cosmetics. She then started a blog about how to save money on cosmetics, which included her shopping tips and many other cosmetics enthusiasts 'suggestions and recommendations. With the increase in visits, she has received the attention and cooperation opportunities of many manufacturers. She can not only try the latest products, but also get lots of lovely gifts for free.

Mr. Tian is a programmer who has a deep interest in numbers and algorithms. This got him bogged down on the worth buying site, where he shuttled through different product pages and found a lot of hidden treasures. By using various promotions and discounts, he saved a lot of money on the items he wanted to buy. His strength is not only in shopping, but also in educating his readers on how to find the most suitable items by optimizing search results and using the coupon codes provided. This not only satisfies his number-loving soul, but also helps many people save a lot of money.

Ms. Liu is an independent musician, she needs to buy some audio and recording equipment in order to better produce music. She found some very good brands and devices on the worth buying website, all at much lower prices than the market. She also wrote a blog post on how to save money on music equipment while shopping. This blog was welcomed and supported by many music producers, and she also gained the attention of many brand manufacturers, and finally was invited to participate in some influential music programs.

Use of secondary markets

Many items do not necessarily need to buy brand new, second-hand market platforms, such as Taobao idle fish, turn around, etc., are good choices. On these platforms, bankrupts can find low-priced second-hand goods that, although they may have some wear and tear, are very cheap. You can use these platforms to exchange for items that meet your needs and save some money.

Case:

Mr. Zhang is in debt because of the failure of his business and is unable to maintain his living necessities. He bought some old appliances and furniture while using idle fish and turning around, and sold items he no longer needed. In this way, Mr. Zhang managed to get out of debt and restart his business.

Ms. Li's husband was unexpectedly unemployed and her family life was under great financial pressure. In order to make a living, she began to turn to idle fish and turn around such platforms to buy necessities of life, while selling items that were no longer needed. After hard work, she successfully got out of the debt quagmire and returned to stable family life.

Mr. Wang owed a large amount of debt due to business losses and failed to ask for help from family and friends. So he took the risk of selling his furniture and some infrequently used items on idle fish and around, and finally managed to get out of trouble by accumulating little by little money.

Ms. Zhang owed a large amount of money for family reasons, but was unable to pay it off. To make a living, she learned to use platforms like idle fish and turn around, saving herself a lot of money by buying depreciated household items. At the same time, she began to clean out the storage room and sell the items she didn't need. Finally, she successfully got out of the quagmire of debt.

Ms. Wang's husband died of illness, leaving huge medical expenses and debts. In order to pay off these debts, she began to sell items that were no longer needed at home on idle fish and around, while living by buying second-hand items to replace the old ones. In this way, she successfully mobilized the power of the community, allowing more people to buy idle items and get out of debt.

Use Tampermonkey plug-in Douban resource download master

It can help users download resources on Douban for free, users can get e-books and movies and other resources for free, to buy expensive physical books, movie tickets and other items. The use method is also very simple, first download Tampermonkey plug-in and install, and then find the watercress resource download master in the Greasy Fork market, after installation, go to the watercress book to find the books you need, the watercress resource download master will recommend the free network disk link to download.

Case:

Xiao Ming is a newly bankrupt entrepreneur, due to economic reasons, he can not buy the required teaching materials, but he is not discouraged, he through the installation of Tampermonkey plug-in, install watercress resources download master, found a free electronic version of PDF books. He acquired knowledge and skills through self-study and eventually found a new job and got out of debt.

Xiao Wang is a high school student who hopes to do well in the college entrance examination, but his family is not rich enough to buy expensive review materials. Fortunately, he found Tampermonkey plug-ins and Douban resource download masters, and by downloading free electronic PDF books, he successfully improved his grades through self-study and was admitted to his favorite university.

Xiao Zhang is a fledgling self-media person who wants to learn more about writing and marketing skills, but his funds are very limited. He learned by downloading free digital PDF books and eventually became a digital marketing expert and made a lot of money.

Xiao Li is an unemployed worker. It is difficult for him to find a good job because of his lack of skills and knowledge. However, through the

Tampermonkey plug-in and Douban resources to download the master, he obtained a free electronic version of the PDF book, and self-taught some skills and knowledge. Eventually, he managed to find a good job and achieved great success in his career.

Xiao Chen is a young mother who wants to play a bigger role in the family, but she lacks the relevant knowledge and skills. By using the Tampermonkey plugin and Douban Resources Download Master, she obtained free electronic PDF books and taught herself a lot about parenting, family management and health. She has successfully elevated her role in the family and has become an excellent mother.

Use Baidu Library Downloader

Baidu Library is an important platform for many people to acquire knowledge, but there is a fee to view the full version of the document. Use Tampermonkey plug-in Baidu library downloader can solve this problem, the tool can download free documents on Baidu library, in order to obtain knowledge at the same time save a certain cost. Find it in the Greasy Fork market of Tampermonkey plugin, you can view and download the complete Baidu library documentation for free!

Case:

Mr. Zhang is heavily in debt due to business failure, and he needs to know about bankruptcy liquidation to protect his rights and interests. However, he found that this information can only be viewed in the VIP members of Baidu Library. Therefore, he downloaded the Tampermonkey plug-in Baidu library downloader, successfully obtained this information, and finally smoothly out of the debt quagmire.

Ms. Nguyen's father was hospitalized and needed to buy expensive drugs for treatment. However, she found that the instructions for these drugs could only be viewed in VIP members of Baidu Library. In order to save money, she downloaded the Tampermonkey plug-in Baidu library downloader, successfully obtained these instructions, successfully treated her father.

Mr. Wang is heavily in debt because he failed to start a company. He needs to know something about debt restructuring to avoid bankruptcy. However, he found that this information can only be viewed in the VIP members of Baidu Library. So he downloaded the Tampermonkey plug-in Baidu library downloader, successfully obtained this information, and finally successfully realized debt restructuring.

Ms. Chen is in financial crisis due to her divorce. She needs to know about the division of property to protect her rights. However, she found that this information can only be viewed in the VIP members of Baidu Library. So she downloaded the Tampermonkey plug-in Baidu library downloader, successfully obtained this information, and finally successfully walked out of the economic crisis.

Mr. Li needs to know relevant legal knowledge to protect his rights and interests due to his involvement in litigation. However, he found that this information can only be viewed in the VIP members of Baidu Library. So he downloaded the Tampermonkey plug-in Baidu library downloader, successfully obtained this information, and finally successfully won the lawsuit.

In short, the online world has many artifacts that can help users save money, and we need to be good at using these tools to reduce unnecessary expenses as much as possible. Hopefully, the methods described in this article will help bankrupts save money and better face the challenges of life.

Actively seek part-time and part-time jobs

With the impact of the economic downturn, more and more people are falling into bankruptcy. As a bankrupt, how can you get out of a difficult situation? Part-time and part-time jobs are a very good option. This article will show you how to take the initiative to find part-time jobs and odd jobs to get out of bankruptcy.

Find your strengths

Everyone has their own strengths and strengths. If you can find your strengths, then you can choose to do work that is related to your strengths. If you don't find your strengths, then immediately learn a simple skill, such as learning, buying a few necessary tools to clean the range hood, dredge the sewer business, you can get two or three hundred dollars at a time. Be sure to do something with a little technical threshold, don't do simple manual labor in exchange for pay, such as pure physical delivery, sorting express delivery. In this way, you can better improve your ability, get more opportunities and higher salary. If you have better skills, such as your strong learning skills, you can get a registered architect/pharmacist certificate and so on, and you can earn tens of thousands of yuan at a time. Or you have a wide network of contacts, learn some real estate sales expertise, help sell second-hand real estate once can get tens of thousands of yuan of generous commission.

Case:

Xiao Li, who has been unable to find a job after graduating from college, tried to earn some pocket money through part-time work. After his own research, he finally chose to clean the range hood. At a price of 150 yuan each, he helped nearby residents clean the range hood. Gradually, he found his advantage and became the most popular range hood cleaning master in the local area.

Xiao opened an electrical repair shop, but because of insufficient funds and experience, business has not been very good. He had learned to repair electrical appliances as an intern at a garage, so he started working part-time as an electrical repairman. He gradually discovered that he had a gift for repairing electrical appliances and enjoyed helping others repair electrical appliances in his spare time. Eventually, he gave up the electrical repair shop and turned into a part-time electrical repairman.

Xiao Wang is a single mother. She quit her job as a manager to take care of her children, but she is under some financial pressure because she has no job. She found herself a part-time job: a registered architect certificate for a construction company. Her credentials enabled her construction company to bid successfully. She now owns her own house and car. She earned all this on the side.

Xiao Yang, who just left the school, is faced with the problem of finding a job after graduation. He learned a lot of practical experience by working part-time as a sewer dredge, no longer relying on financial support from his family. He's so popular now that his phone rings every day.

Xiao Feng has been in the advertising industry, but after the company's transformation deducted his commission bonus. He felt very lost, and at the same time understood that life without income was unrealistic. He began to accept part-time tasks for advertising companies to install outdoor advertising, and eventually he improved the quality of the installation for three companies and became one of the top installation masters in the industry.

Xiao Li was originally a long-term unemployed person, passed the examination to obtain a pharmacist certificate, attached to a registered pharmacist certificate to a newly opened drugstore. He also found a new job and got double pay. In the past few months, he has earned enough money to buy a car.

Xiao Jiang is facing financial problems at home. She wants to find a part-time job close to home and with high income. She started selling second-hand houses, earning a commission from them. Now, she has become one of the local middlemen and proudly owns her own house.

Cheng found his advantage. He was good at installing air conditioners as a part-time job. His income is very good, especially in the summer! The payment for installing air conditioners has helped to improve the quality of life.

Xiao Wei is a freelance writer whose writing style is highly recognized. He created a Weixin Official Accounts and gradually accumulated many fans. Now, he makes content for his public account every day and earns a lot of money through Tencent's advertising alliance.

Xiao used to be a primary school teacher, but he faced many physical problems because of his long working hours. He found a part-time job that matched his physical condition:One-on-one tutoring for the children of wealthy businessmen at another elite school. And earned a good income. He can now take better care of his body while earning the income he wants.

Find ways to provide value to society

Bankruptcies need to look at people's lives to find their pain points. Some problems or needs may not be met in the market, such as difficult internship for students, transportation for the elderly, etc., while some pain points are existing problems in the market, but still need to be further solved. For example, some elderly people feel that family pension is not enough and need to participate in social activities. At this time, the bankrupt needs to focus on the customer pain point and fully understand the customer's voice and needs in order to develop innovative, solving and competitive products or services. Find the path of entrepreneurship, that is, the direction and way of entrepreneurship. They can choose their own areas of expertise and a high degree of understanding of the existing market areas, through specific market research and analysis to understand customer needs and market conditions. For bankrupts without any business background, they can start from a small range of income, such as breeding pet cats at home to sell, and then expand the scale of breeding, in order to get rid of the debt quagmire.

Case:

After Xiao Ming went bankrupt, he observed the market and found that some young people had a demand for fitness but had limited time. As a result, he created an online smart fitness platform that tailored professional fitness programs for users and won a broad user base.

After her business failure, Xiao Hong found that many young people needed to learn career skills but had no chance. She started an online vocational education institution that provides vocational skills training and career planning guidance, helping many young people find jobs and boost their incomes.

Xiao Li opened a pastry shop with all his money, but there was little business. He aimed at the living needs of women in the community, changed his business model, cooperated with the community to deliver goods to home, won the trust and love of female customers, and finally developed the pastry shop into a baking chain enterprise.

Xiao Zhang was in financial trouble and began to work part-time and provide services on the Internet instead. He used his skills as a programmer to develop a diagnostic tool for hardware facilities, and provided free technical support and repair guides on many forums and online skill sharing platforms, winning a lot of free publicity and eventually successfully switching from online part-time to physical store operations.

Xiao Liu's economy is unbalanced, but he makes a living selling honey in his circle of friends. He observed that rural beekeepers in many places were very backward in the way they stored and sold honey, so he improved the storage and sales strategy for rural beekeepers, further expanded the sales market, and successfully got rid of the debt problem.

Small money is in short supply, but he observes that office supplies procurement costs for small and medium-sized enterprises in big cities are getting higher and higher, so he opened an online platform for wholesale and retail of office supplies, and established close cooperation with manufacturers and logistics companies to reduce costs and become a stable supplier for many offices.

After Xiao Dong went bankrupt, he began to use his spare time to help the elderly solve various problems encountered in life, such as shopping, seeing a doctor, repairing, etc., which won a lot of praise and recognition. He officially started as a counselor for the elderly, focusing on this fast-growing population base and adding new selling points accordingly, becoming an online platform for providing pension services for the elderly.

After the bankruptcy of small orders, focus on innovative aquatic product planting technology. He has developed a special method for raising shellfish, which makes a perfect transition between the traditional production technology of "dry and fresh" and automated farming equipment on his own small piece of water. By helping others to change their own thoughts and habits, he continues to launch new brands and win a large number of consumers in the market.

After Xiaolan went bankrupt, she paid attention to observing women's body-shaping needs. Considering that women have to balance a lot of work and life needs in modern people's daily life, she opened a massage parlor, which catered to the demand of modern women's consumer market for body shaping and created a brand-new market segment.

Xiao Yao appeared after bankruptcy, devoted himself to studying the demographic data of local small cities, delved into various business models, finally locked in the market with education service and employment as the core, and established an online teaching information platform for logistics distribution and training. He pulled himself out of bankruptcy by successfully solving the employment problem.

Don't lose face and be afraid of hardship

Smile and face life with confidence. Before you do anything, think about what you want to achieve, what you need to do to achieve it, and how much time and effort you need to put into it. In the process of doing things, don't complain and complain, do it with your heart and cherish every opportunity.

Case:

A bankrupt businessman arrives in a small city and finds a part-time job as a cashier at the local supermarket. Although his salary was low, he worked hard and eventually saved enough money to pay off his debts after a few months.

An unemployed young man who had taken out a lot of money at high interest rates decided to take up a job as a back rub when the debt became an unbearable burden. Although the job was very tiring, he managed to pay off his debts within a few months.

A small business goes bankrupt because of poor performance, and the owner loses all his savings and can't pay his debts. In order to pay off his debts, he opened a small restaurant and managed it seriously. After two years of hard work, he finally earned enough money to pay off his debts.

A retired man spends all his savings on illegal high-yield investments and ends up in huge debt. Although he was old, the old man realized that he should be responsible for his mistakes and chose to work as a cleaner to earn money to pay off his debts.

A real estate agent went bankrupt due to a broken capital chain, and he had to work as a worker in a local factory. Although it was a drudge job, he worked hard and eventually paid off his debts and returned to his industry.

A laborer takes out a loan to buy a house while working hard to make money, and ends up in radical debt. He moved to work at the local garbage station, working as a city cleaner, and he eventually paid off his debts.

A "small rich is safe" life of the rich second generation, in the original "Xanadu" life can not help themselves, but also owed a huge debt. Finally, he came to the market as a vegetable vendor and worked hard to pay off all his debts.

A frustrated young talent because of escape debt desperate, found an online store customer service job, and stubbornly worked for two years, conscientious, never lazy, finally reluctantly paid off the debt.

In short, part-time jobs and odd jobs are a good way to help you with your financial problems. However, to be successful, you need to find your own strengths, find ways to provide value to society, not afraid of hardship, full of confidence. I believe that as long as you bravely take the first step, you will be able to find your own piece of heaven and earth in part-time and part-time jobs.

Ideas and methods of independent entrepreneurship and sideline

In recent years, as the economy has faltered, many have found themselves plunged into bankruptcy. In this case, exploring independent entrepreneurship and sideline has become the choice of many people, but bankrupts are not the only entrepreneurs, and there are already many successful businesses and individuals in the market. Therefore, it is particularly important to find ideas and methods for independent entrepreneurship and sideline.

Abandon interests and hobbies, respect the market

Don't start from your own interests or hobbies, but from the perspective of the market. When looking for independent entrepreneurship and sideline, bankrupts should first consider the market demand of today's society, understand the development trend of the market and potential business opportunities. Only by understanding the market demand can we find the right business opportunities in the market.

Case:

Xiao Zhang has always loved reading. He thought it was his dream to open a bookstore, so he spent all his savings to open a bookstore. He did not consider the market demand and competition, but simply believed that his interest could attract enough customers. However, with the rise of e-books and competition from large chain bookstores, Xiao Zhang's bookstore has become increasingly depressed. Eventually he took out more loans to stay afloat and went bankrupt.

Xiao Li liked playing games very much when he was a child. When he grew up, he decided to open a game company, thinking that his game concept could attract many players. However, he did not do enough market research and did not realize how competitive the market was. Due to heavy investment and insufficient sales, the company fell into a state of loss and eventually went bankrupt with high debts.

Xiao Wang has always been a fashion lover, he felt that opening a small shop selling jewelry is a very meaningful thing. He only chooses and buys goods according to his personal interests, relying on his reputation and experience to attract more consumers. But he didn't anticipate the lack of awareness of his brand, which led to declining sales, growing losses and eventual closure.

Xiao Zhao has always loved food and has always dreamed of opening his own restaurant. He first quit, then found a suitable position and hired some cooks and waiters to start the restaurant. He had thought that his skills were sufficient, but he did not expect that the customer's taste was not entirely in line with his own. Due to operational problems and mismanagement, it eventually caused serious cash flow problems and eventually went bankrupt.

He loves coffee, so he decided to open his own coffee shop. He spent a lot of time and money decorating the store and buying a lot of high-quality coffee beans. However, he didn't choose a good location, didn't do enough market research, coffee was hard to sell, and no one knew where his coffee shop was. With a limited customer base and lower-than-expected store sales, he was eventually forced to close.

Mr. Zhang is a young man who loves music. He is destined to make his way in the music industry. So he took out all his debt and invested in a new musical instrument supply store. He didn't do enough market research and thought that having a good product was enough to win the market. However, what Zhang did not foresee was that there were plenty of competitors in the market and consumers were more willing to buy cheaper products. His business eventually went bankrupt, leaving him with a huge debt.

Miss Li's dream is to open a Hanfu shop. She didn't do enough research in the market, just considering her and her friends 'love for Hanfu, she went all out to open a store. At first she seemed to be successful, but she later found it difficult to make money in the business. Her Hanfu store was too limited to consumers and soon faced huge debts.

Uncle Wang wants to build a store that serves high-end tea. He believes that if the quality of his drinks is higher, the revenue will be higher, and consumers will give some recognition and support. So he began his investment journey, unaware that most of the customers in the market would prefer to buy cheaper drinks. Uncle Wang's tea shop eventually closed down and he fell into huge debt.

Mr. Liu fell in love with mahjong and decided to open a mahjong parlor in the industry. He invested all his money and, guided by his interests, developed a business strategy and sales plan. However, he ignored the brutal competition in the market and the changes in consumer demand. Soon, his sales dropped, the store's prospects of making money were slim, and he was in a desperate situation.

Ask for help from friends with resources

Bankruptcies should be aware of their network, ask questions and get advice from people with social resources (such as government officials, entrepreneurs, self-employed bosses). They may need you to help them do something profitable but troublesome! This is a rare opportunity for you. In the process of starting a business, network resources play a pivotal role, by expanding their network circle, making it easier for them to access valuable information and resources. At the same time, bankrupts need to know how to use their network resources, how to get help and support from these people, so that they can develop more smoothly.

Case:

Mr. Chen felt deeply lost after bankruptcy and wanted to give up countless times. But he was not willing to let it go, so he began to ask his friends for help. One of his friends is a government official in a certain place. After many exchanges, the government officials gave Mr. Chen an opportunity to develop agricultural products. After hard work, Mr. Chen organized a team and began to do research with the local government, and finally launched his own brand in the local area.

Ms. Xu was originally an entrepreneur, but later due to the outbreak of swine fever, her pig farm went bankrupt together, she had no confidence in the future, began to travel around the world, looking for a new way out of life. On a trip, Ms. Xu met a successful entrepreneur who suggested Ms. Xu to do compound fertilizer. After many considerations, Ms. Xu finally decided to follow the entrepreneur's suggestion to try new things. After years of hard work, she achieved her own new enterprise.

Mr. ruo used to be very successful in business, but in recent years his company went bankrupt. He began to constantly look for opportunities to ask for help from capable people around him, and found that an old friend had become an executive at a famous Internet company. He began to keep in touch with the company, eventually getting orders from the company, and a few years later, with the company's support, Mr. Ruo began to build his new store.

Xiao Wu used to be in charge of the management of the machinery department in a state-owned enterprise. However, as the market shifted, the original company faced a lot of pressure and began to go bankrupt. Xiao Wu lost confidence in his future, so he began to ask his friends for help. A friend introduced his management work of a supply chain company. With his own management experience, Xiao Wu became an important backbone in the company, honed himself step by step, and finally started to start a business and became his own boss.

Kobayashi ran a small restaurant in a certain area, but for financial reasons, he had to give up the business and went bankrupt. Frustrated, Kobayashi decided to seek help from his entrepreneur friends. His friends told him that a company was planning to go public and needed a restaurant as the basis for an expansion plan. Because Kobayashi had a wealth of dining experience, his friends gave him the opportunity and soon succeeded in pushing the restaurant to the capital market.

Mr. Liu is a retired science and technology worker. He started his own company, but it went bankrupt because of the pressure of competition in the market. After going bankrupt, his friends in the government offered him a chance. He told him that his city was focusing on developing high-tech industries and needed a company to develop and produce independently innovative products. Mr. Liu was invited to participate and successfully took control of the company, which became one of the driving forces behind the city's economic development.

Mr. Liu was a manager of an insurance company, but his company had to close down because of the economic depression. After going bankrupt, his entrepreneur friends offered him another chance. He told him that his company was expanding into commodity trading and needed an insurance company to cover it. Mr. Liu accepted the opportunity and succeeded in becoming one of the leading enterprises in this field.

Mr. Wang is a manager of a traditional textile company, but the company lost its competitive advantage due to market competition and insufficient product renewal speed. After going bankrupt, his entrepreneur friend offered him a way out. He told him that he was looking for an innovative company to help him develop a new product that could have a wide market demand in the world market. Mr. Wang accepted this task and was included in the development team, and finally successfully developed this new product, which became the inexhaustible driving force for the company's innovation and development.

Mr. Chen was a doctor, but his private hospital went bankrupt because of mismanagement. After going bankrupt, his government friends offered him a chance. He told him that their city was aggressively exploring the health and wellness market and needed a company with the strength and money to develop and deliver such services. Mr. Chen accepted the opportunity and successfully established a new company to become one of the promoters of the development of emerging markets.

Don't innovate easily

Bankruptcies need to understand that most innovation is a deep hole, so bankrupts can't afford to take that risk. Therefore, in the process of looking for independent entrepreneurship and sideline, it is better to follow the success of the market, copy it, compete with it, and surpass it. Why would you do that? Don't feel ashamed, because this method will allow you to avoid detours, reduce the risk of failure, and have a higher probability of success. For example, if you want to open a restaurant, where should it be located? Is it a blank market around the new community? Absolutely not! The best location is next door to the very popular restaurant! Think carefully about the reason.

Case:

Mr. Zhang, a former owner of a small business, lost all his assets and credibility as problems such as a shrinking market and mismanagement led to the bankruptcy of the business. After a period of precipitation, Mr. Zhang started his business again. Instead of innovating, however, he found the most successful competitor in the market and copied his product and business model. Through unremitting efforts and good marketing strategies, he not only reopened the market, but also won the recognition and trust of customers.

Ms. Li is a former designer of famous brands. She lost her job and her reputation as a result of the company's poor management and design. A few years later, she resumed her entrepreneurial journey. However, she did not choose to innovate or find new market opportunities. Using the designs she created that year, and successfully copying similar products from the market and imitating them, she successfully earned back her past economic status and honor.

Wang was a business manager at a small technology company, but the company failed to keep up with technological advances and mismanagement led to its bankruptcy. A few years later, he started his own business. However, instead of trying new technological innovations or looking for other market opportunities, he learned from the innovations and management ideas of other successful companies in the market and copied them into his new company. His company quickly became profitable and growing.

Ms. Zhang used to be an accountant, but she lost her job and reputation because of the company's internal management chaos and financial mistakes. A few years later, Ms. Zhang resumed her entrepreneurial journey. However, instead of innovating or trying new market opportunities, she copied the financial management of other successful companies. By learning and imitating the experiences and success stories in the market, she discovered unique and successful methods and started her own profitable journey with them.

Xiao Li was the owner of a famous restaurant, but he went bankrupt because of mismanagement and mismanagement. After a long period of pain and self-reflection, he finally realized his mistake and decided to pull himself together again. This time, he gave up on his own innovative ideas and instead went to study restaurants that were successful in the market. By imitating and refining the methods he learned, he succeeded in building a popular restaurant and earning the respect and trust of the market.

Xiao Wang is a young online shop owner, but despite his creativity and enthusiasm, his start-up has not been recognized by the market. He often studies the experiences of industry leaders and then translates their wisdom into his own ideas to improve products and services. Through continuous learning and improvement, Xiao Wang eventually created a market-leading online store, and received praise from the majority of users.

Xiao Chen is a young IT engineer whose role in startups is not obvious. But he didn't give up. He always studied technology companies that were successful in the market and analyzed their technologies and services. Gradually, he learned what methods and tools could help them succeed in the marketplace. Through collaboration with industry leaders and fierce competition, Xiao Chen eventually built a software that was popular in the market and became one of the leading companies in the industry.

Xiao Zhang is a young independent designer whose design works are full of creativity and self-style, but have not been recognized by the market. He decided to study the designers who were successful in the market and learn their design methods and thought processes. Gradually, he succeeded in gaining market recognition, becoming a highly sought after designer and achieving excellence in his field.

Kobayashi is a young entrepreneur who has failed in startups. He learned his lesson and realized that his failure was due to lack of market research and unfamiliarity with his competitors. So he began to learn about successful companies in the market and understand their market research and marketing strategies. Through his tireless efforts in a highly competitive market, he eventually became a successful entrepreneur, leading an award-winning company.

Looking for an investment or partner

Bankruptcies should try their best to obtain investment or find partners when starting a business, reduce their investment ratio and reduce risks. In the case of a shortage of funds, bankrupts to obtain venture capital is indeed a very difficult thing. Partnering with others, or seeking investment from others, gives you more options for capital, reduces your investment ratio, and reduces risk. With a little more labor and effort, and success, you'll have the capital you need for your next venture.

Case:

Mr. Wang suffered heavy losses in his last venture, but he didn't give up, but learned the lesson of failure. This time he found several partners to pool the money and develop the latest product. Through a well-crafted marketing plan, they succeeded in breaking into the market and making huge profits.

Ms. Wang has gone bankrupt before, but she has learned her lesson. This time she didn't choose to put all her money into the venture, but looked for investors. Her plan was backed by an experienced investor who successfully took the company to new heights through smart business and marketing strategies.

Mr. Zhang is a visionary entrepreneur. He invented a new product and launched a massive publicity campaign. Although he didn't have much money at first, he managed to bring the product to market by attracting investors and partners. Now he has enough capital to start his next venture.

Mr. Zhang is an entrepreneur engaged in the catering industry. He once ran a restaurant called Taste Xuan, but went bankrupt because of a broken capital chain. After much deliberation, Mr. Zhang decided to start from scratch. Instead of going it alone, he expanded his social circle and formed a new restaurant brand with a group of like-minded people. They invested enough money and developed a detailed marketing plan and operation plan. With high quality products, good service and reasonable price, they quickly gained a good reputation and wide recognition in the local market.

Ms. Wang is an entrepreneur who runs a clothing store. Although she suffered some setbacks in her previous entrepreneurial attempts, she did not give up. At the same time, she didn't reinvest all her personal money in the new project. Instead, she found several investors and showed them her business plan. These investors were impressed by her determination, expertise, and hard work, and were willing to invest in her cause. Under her leadership, the team members worked together to achieve impressive results in advertising and promotion, and established their brand image in the market.

Mr. Li is a young IT entrepreneur. He once entered the market as the founder of an online travel company, but the company closed after years of operation due to mismanagement. Instead of backing down, however, he took the opportunity to see his weaknesses and seek out good partners to make up for them. In terms of money, he did not put all his manpower and resources into a new project. Instead, he started raising capital and built a solid foundation for some key businesses, thereby minimizing risk. This time, he finally succeeded and developed the company into a well-known brand that won the trust of customers.

Ms. Zhang is a self-employed entrepreneur who runs a fruit shop. Her business started very well, but because she was too eager to expand the size of the store without adequate financial planning and budget, the store was operating at a loss. Seeing this, she decided to put the project on hold and seek more business advice and partners. Today, her small store has opened again and gained a certain reputation in the community, but this time she did not impulsively expand the size of the store, but paid more attention to consumer demand, paid attention to marketing strategy, and learned from other successful stores to achieve sustainable profitability.

Use new technology to combine traditional industries

Bankruptcies should closely follow the development trend of new technologies, use new technologies to combine traditional industries, and gain the ability to surpass most players in traditional industries. Technological progress is inevitable, and all walks of life are facing the impact of new technologies. Therefore, bankrupts need to keep an eye on the latest technology trends in the market and combine these new technologies with their entrepreneurial projects to better gain market recognition.

Case:

Mr. Wang is a boss who has been in the electronics industry for many years, but after Mr. Wang's business went bankrupt, he found that the traditional electronics industry had been flooded. Therefore, Mr. Wang decided to combine the electronics industry with high-tech such as smart home and began to develop a new generation of smart home products. He added biometric technology and smart home control system to the product, making the smart home product more functional and more in line with customer needs. Now, Mr. Wang's enterprise has risen again and become a leader in the field of smart home.

Ms. Zhang is a boss who has been committed to exploring how to make customers enjoy the ultimate experience in the furniture industry. But after going through a bankruptcy, she thinks the traditional furniture industry has been overwhelmed by countless furniture factories. Therefore, Ms. Zhang combines furniture and intelligent technology, injects smart home control system and Internet of Things technology into the product, and provides brand-new home design concept, which not only pays attention to beauty and comfort, but also is very intelligent, which can better promote people's living experience. Now, Ms. Zhang's furniture store business is booming, becoming a leader in the field of home customization.

Mr. Wu is a boss who has been through industrial automation for many years. After a bankruptcy, he thinks his traditional industry has not crossed the gap of the times. Therefore, Mr. Wu considered combining industrial automation technology with intelligent hardware and developed a brand-new workplace safety monitoring and identification system, which not only improved the degree of automation, but also improved the quality and efficiency of production line by using a large amount of data analysis and artificial intelligence. Now, Mr. Wu's business has regained its success and become one of the famous enterprises in the field of industrial automation.

Mr. Sun is a boss who has been in the logistics field for many years, but he finds that traditional industries can no longer meet market demand. Sun decided to combine the logistics field with the latest blockchain technology to build a complete logistics management platform to make the logistics industry more efficient and transparent. By using modern technology to intelligently search and manage the location of goods, product leakage and loss are reduced, resulting in better customer satisfaction, bringing more business and greater profitability to Mr. Sun's business.

Mr. Wang was the owner of a theater, but his theater was greatly challenged by the changing market, which eventually led to bankruptcy. However, Mr. Wang did not give up. After his bankruptcy, he decided to start a new business. He decided to combine traditional theatrical performances with the latest technology and launched a new product called "VR Theater". With this product, users can watch the performance on the stage as if they were in an actual theater. The product has performed very well in the market and Mr. Wang has regained his success

Mr. Zhang is the owner of a traditional restaurant, but because of the changes in the market, his store is increasingly difficult to attract customers. To gain a competitive edge, Mr. Zhang decided to combine traditional dining with the latest technology. He introduced a new service called "smart ordering," in which customers can use their phones to scan QR codes on their tables to order and pay, eliminating the need to wait for waiters to serve and check out. The service was well received by customers, and Mr. Zhang was able to start his own business again.

Ms. Wang is the owner of a traditional clothing store, but with the rise of e-commerce, it is increasingly difficult for her store to get enough traffic. To gain a competitive edge, Ms. Wang decided to combine traditional clothing with the latest technology and launched a new service called "virtual fitting room". With this service, customers can try on clothes at home via mobile APP, upload their photos to the APP, and then use the virtual fitting room function to try on different styles of clothing. The service brought a lot of new customers to her store, and Ms. Wang regained her competitive edge in the market.

Mr. Liu is the owner of a traditional coffee shop, but because of the changing market, his store is increasingly difficult to attract customers. To gain a competitive edge, Liu decided to combine traditional coffee shops with the latest technology. He introduced a new device called the Smart Coffee Maker, where customers can use a mobile APP to customize their coffee flavor and make it automatically on the smart coffee maker. The service was so popular with customers that Mr. Liu successfully fended off fierce competition in the market.

Ms. Li is the owner of a traditional bookstore, but her store is increasingly struggling to attract customers because of the popularity of e-books. To gain a competitive edge, Ms. Li decided to combine traditional bookstores with the latest technology. She joined an e-platform called Online Bookstore, which offers customers a range of high-quality books that they can buy and read online. The service succeeded in attracting a large number of users, and Ms. Li regained her competitive edge in the market.

Outsource everything that can be outsourced

Bankruptcies should focus on their core capabilities and outsource non-core capabilities through social division of labor to reduce resource costs. Bankruptcies have relatively limited resources, so if they can use external resources, they can better meet market demand under limited conditions. This is also very necessary.

Case:

Somewhere in Guangdong, China, there is a construction boss named Li Ming. His company used to be the leading enterprise in this area, but due to market changes and repeated mistakes in business strategy, the company gradually weakened and fell into trouble. However, Li Ming did not give up. During this time, he learned from construction companies around the world, thought hard, and decided to re-enter the construction industry.

In the process of starting over, Li Ming learned a new way of doing business-outsourcing. He focused the company on the project itself and outsourced the design, construction and other work, effectively reducing costs. At the same time, he drew on the experience of other companies, constantly improving the existing business and improving work efficiency. Through painstaking efforts, Li Ming has successfully completed a number of projects, involving industrial, commercial, residential and other fields. He began to gradually out of the predicament, through their own efforts and experience, successfully embarked on the road to revival.

Mr. Li is the boss of a printing company. Due to fierce market competition and mismanagement, the company began to go bankrupt. Mr. Li knew very well that if he did not take action, his company would soon be out of the printing market. So he started thinking about some new business models. Mr. Li found a design company in the market, they are willing to provide design services for Mr. Li, and follow some specific requirements. This decision has greatly reduced the financial pressure on the company, and Mr. Li no longer needs to hire designers alone. At the same time, it also enhances the company's production process and realizes more refined service through outsourcing. Mr. Li's company has re-established its position in the highly competitive market by re-aligning its business and providing quality design services and high-quality prints to new and existing customers.

Mr. Wang is an industry insider engaged in the property industry for many years. He always dreamed of starting his own business and having his own property company. So, in an opportunity, he used all his savings to start a property company. At the beginning, Mr. Wang's property company had a difficult time, because the company not only contracted property management work, but also was responsible for low-end work such as security, cleaning and maintenance, and needed to pay for all employees 'salaries, insurance and benefits. At the same time, all kinds of expenses keep pouring in, so that the company's profits are in trouble, even on the verge of bankruptcy. But Mr. Wang did not give up. He was well aware of his weaknesses and believed that the company's earnings needed to be fundamentally changed. So he began to study the strategy of bidding. He restructured his company to focus on property management as its core business. Other low-end jobs such as security, cleaning and maintenance are all outsourced, saving a lot of costs and increasing the company's profits. After the change, Mr. Wang's company ushered in a wave of new opportunities. Through competitive price, he won more contract projects and laid a solid foundation for the company's future development. In the end, Mr. Wang's company embarked on the road to success and became a leader in the property management industry.

Mr. Li's education career was also at a low ebb. He has taught many students to do math and has a good reputation in the hearts of students and parents, but he is under financial pressure to find a more effective model. He began online training and found an educational consultancy to outsource his summer math classes. This Olympiad class is taught by a teacher from another educational institution. Teacher Li only needs to provide support in terms of venue, enrollment, marketing, etc. He soon found that his new business model was a quick success because students and parents still wanted to learn math, the outsourcing agency provided advanced teaching methods to make the course more interesting, and Li continued to expand this market share through his marketing knowledge.

Mr. Wang and his studio went bankrupt. He used to be a well-known photographer, but his business went downhill due to fierce competition in the market. But for a while, his business wasn't doing so well. He thought about a lot of solutions, including improving quality and lowering prices, but none worked well. Mr Wang doesn't want to give up. He wants to bounce back and create new products that appeal to customers. But he also realized that he didn't want to bear the cost of hiring. Mr. Wang thought of a new way:Outsource these operations to provide only studio space and focus more on marketing. So he signed a collaboration agreement with a photographer and a makeup artist. His studio became the place where they worked. As Mr. Wang focused on marketing, he successfully promoted these cooperative businesses. While reducing the cost of expenses, his partners also made more money. This kind of cooperation is accepted by many photographers and makeup artists and is widely used. Mr. Wang has also become a new winner.

In a small city in Henan Province, there is a car repair shop called Mr.

Li. Mr. Li is a well-known car repairman in the city, but in 2015, his store suffered a business crisis and went bankrupt due to a downturn in the auto market and poor management. But Mr. Li didn't give up. He took his tools and skills and restored a new store. This time he wanted to do a more elaborate operation. Instead of hiring, he formed a partnership with some of the maintenance workers who had worked in his store in the past, outsourcing the maintenance work to a receptionist who would guard the door. This approach paid off quickly, as he reduced his expenses, focused more on maintaining relationships with insurance companies, and secured more repair orders. This more than tripled Mr. Li's business and helped him out of the woods.

Ms. Wang used to run an IT training company. In order to improve the experience and quality of her students 'courses, she needed to buy a lot of computer equipment and software, but the high price of these equipment and software would put a heavy burden on her company. Ms. Wang sprouted the idea of renting computers. Working with a local computer rental company, Ms. Wang rents a PC for each student, while using the software's agent license to keep costs to a minimum. In this way, Ms. Wang has succeeded in reducing the cost of her company, while greatly improving the satisfaction and service quality of her students.

In short, finding independent businesses and side businesses is a good opportunity for bankrupts to get back on their feet. However, in this process, bankrupts still need to keep calm, from the market point of view, access to market information and opportunities, at the same time, good at dealing with interpersonal relationships, make a wider network of contacts, in order to obtain more resources and help, and finally can achieve their own development goals.

Social media based marketing and promotion

With the current instability of economic development and the impact of the epidemic, more and more enterprises and individuals have fallen into financial difficulties and even faced bankruptcy. However, bankruptcy does not mean that the road to entrepreneurship of enterprises or individuals is over. On the contrary, it is most important to re-choose the appropriate direction and strategy.

How to promote and market your new business based on social media? Here are a few suggestions:

Identify the target audience

To promote and market your new business on social media platforms, you first need to know who your target audience is. Which group? Doing so helps to better target their needs and preferences, providing more engaging content and information, which increases attention and conversion rates.

For example, if your new business is aimed at young people, you can choose to promote it on well-known social media platforms for young people, such as Weibo, Douyin, Little Red Book, etc.;If your new business is enterprise-oriented, you can choose to promote it on LinkedIn. Depending on the audience, choosing the right social media platform can be more effective in promoting and marketing.

Case:

A young man found a new restaurant on Weibo. Attracted by the restaurant's youthful decor and food signs, he shared photos and comments on his microblog. This Weibo post was forwarded and liked by his friends who followed him. The restaurant's exposure on Weibo was greatly increased, attracting more young people to patronize.

There is an emerging online education platform that has posted Short videos tutorials on chatter, attracting the attention and learning of many young people. These videos have been highly played and praised on the vibrato, and the brand awareness of the company has increased, and it has also successfully promoted its new business.

There is a young fashion blogger who shares his clothes and cosmetics on Little Red Book. She has a huge fan base, spreading the latest trends in fashion and beauty on Little Red Book, attracting many young women who also love beauty. Therefore, some beauty brands began to contact her in the small red book cooperation promotion, successfully promoted their products.

One young man started a cultural media company and posted his company profile and job listings on LinkedIn. Because LinkedIn's users are more business and professional, he received applications from serious and willing job seekers, as well as business partners who contacted him, and the company expanded rapidly.

There is a newly established start-up company, in the pulse released its own entrepreneurial projects and team introduction. Because the user group of Pulse is mainly professionals and entrepreneurs, many investors and people in the same industry soon paid attention to and consulted the company, and the company also actively cooperated with other enterprises through Pulse.

New business promotion

Once the target audience is identified, the next step is to promote your new business so that more people know, understand and accept it.

At this time, it is recommended to send some interesting and valuable articles, photos, videos, etc. on social media to attract users 'attention. At the same time, with some short and lean text description, highlight the characteristics and selling points of the new business.

In addition, some interactive marketing means, such as lottery, punch card, etc., can also be adopted to increase the participation and forwarding volume of users as much as possible, and improve the exposure of new business.

Case:

In a small town in Fujian, a young man opened an online celebrity shop specializing in cartoon-themed desserts. He built the store near famous tourist attractions and posted photos of the finished product on social media, attracting many young tourists to taste it and becoming a local online store.

An e-commerce company in Guangdong has launched a raffle on

social media to attract more young audiences for a new specialty. Participants are required to share the company's promotion within a specified time and upload photos of themselves tasting the food to win the grand prize.

A well-known restaurant chain has opened a brand-new branch in Beijing, and in order to let consumers know the features and selling points of the new store, they have released a series of video advertisements on social media. Through videos showing different cooking techniques and ingredients, the restaurants have attracted many young people with a passion for food

A gym in Shanghai has launched a new team exercise class, and they have posted an introductory video of the class, a trainer training video and photos of participants on social media. The gym successfully attracted many new users through videos and photos showing the passion and sports fun of the coaches and Ying Zongtian.

A restaurant company in Beijing has opened a new wine store. As they promote the new store, they posted a punch-card event on Weibo, where participants posted posts while taking photos with a smile. They then put together a video of the card and posted it on social media platforms. This has attracted many users and small partners to punch cards and taste wine in the store.

Wang is an indie game developer who blogs on social media about the progress of his latest game. In the blog, he shares many interesting stories and tips from the game development process, along with some screenshots and highlights of the game. The blog was loved and followed by many gamers and indie game developers, helping Wang's new game gain more exposure on social media and attract more users.

Lili is a mobile app developer who is working on a new app that will help people better manage their time and work. In order to attract more target users, Lili posted a series of tips and suggestions on time management, productivity and other aspects on social media, as well as sharing some interesting stories and experiences she encountered in developing applications. The content immediately drew attention and response from social media users, and attracted many new users to download her app.

Build a social circle

Social media is a social platform, and building a good social circle is also the key to promotion and marketing. Therefore, on social media, you can actively interact with people and build your own social circle in which to share, interact and promote your new business.

At the same time, you can also join some relevant groups or communities, interact with some peers or potential customers, communicate and learn from each other in order to better understand the market, identify opportunities, increase exposure and promote conversion.

Case:

Zhang Xiaolong works as a waiter in a fast food restaurant, but he always has his own ideas and ideas. One day, his friend invited him to start a restaurant together. Zhang Xiaolong was responsible for menu research and store design, while his friend was responsible for operation management. Their restaurant focuses on healthy eating and promotes it on social media platforms. Thanks to Zhang Xiaolong's dexterity and creative menu, the restaurant quickly became a local favorite.

Li Jing, a laid-off bank employee, feels lost and at a loss. But she has always had a soft spot for jewelry design, so she began to teach herself about jewelry design and began posting her work on social media platforms. She quickly gained a lot of fans, established a brand of her own online and became a popular Jewelry designer.

Wang Jun is a programmer, and his company went bankrupt for some reason. He dreamed of doing something fun, so he started researching VR technology and developing his own VR gaming platform. At the same time, he also published his own VR games on social media platforms and shared experiences and communication with netizens. He quickly gained some loyal fans and led to more investment in his start-up.

Mr. Zhao has done countless manual jobs, but as he sought to improve his quality of life, he began investing in making handbags. He saw custom totes as a product that had a market demand, so he started promoting his products on social media platforms and connecting with customers, sharing his work history and production skills. Thanks to his hard work and patience, he soon became a popular handbag manufacturer.

Wang Lei is an ordinary cleaner, as boring as his job. He has always been interested in football clothing design, so he began to study and develop his own design projects. He used his knowledge and communication on social media platforms to share his work and connect with customers, which quickly worked. His football clothing designs were very popular, winning a series of awards and market share, and creating his own brand.

Improve customer service

Social media is not only a platform for promotion and marketing, but also a platform for customer service. Therefore, while promoting and marketing new business, we should always pay attention to the feedback and needs of users, actively respond to users 'questions and complaints, and provide all-round customer service.

Effective customer service can increase customer loyalty and increase their satisfaction, which in turn increases exposure and conversion rates for new business.

Case:

Li Xiaohong lost her job because her company went bankrupt, but she didn't give up. She has created a small shop on social media that sells handmade and exquisite accessories. She actively responds to customer feedback and promptly responds to customer questions and complaints through WeChat circle of friends. Her attentive service and high quality products have won many loyal customers.

Zhang Ming because of the impact of the epidemic, his restaurant is facing the crisis of closure. But he couldn't accept defeat. He uses social media to provide recipes, instructional videos and interactions for clients. He also organizes online activities on social media, such as cooking in the air, to keep interacting with customers. His service and innovation have won the love of many consumers, which has increased the exposure and conversion rate of the restaurant.

Zhao Lijuan worked in an electronics company for more than 10 years, because the company failed to operate properly, she decided to set up her own door. She runs a beauty salon on social media and shares her beauty tips and experiences with customers via live video. Her professional ability and considerate service make her get more and more customers 'recognition and praise, bring more business and profit.

Wang Qiang and Li Hua are a couple who have been running a small supermarket for more than 10 years. However, during the epidemic, their supermarkets encountered sales bottlenecks. To break through, they use social media platforms to offer customers more services and coupons, such as free home delivery and healthy food recommendations. These services can meet the needs and expectations of customers, attract more and more consumers, and obtain more new customers through word of mouth from former loyal customers.

Ma Fei is a freelancer who is passionate about travel and photography. As the impact of the epidemic cost her a lucrative job as a tour guide and travel photographer, she decided to create a blog on social media to share the tourist areas, routes and photography techniques that inspired her. She actively responded to readers 'questions, continuously expanded the content direction, improved the quality, attracted the attention and love of the target readers, and finally succeeded in winning the favor of advertisements and sponsors, realizing her dream.

Luo Xiaolong is a mobile game planner, and his mobile game team went bankrupt due to poor management. Luo Xiaolong is thinking, if can let the user participate in game making process better, so such game will be more popular. He began to listen carefully to user feedback, constantly revising game planning, timely release of game updates and customer support services. Now, his mobile game has become a story in the industry and has become a favorite of many young people.

Xiong Xiaojuan, a fashion designer, went bankrupt because of the epidemic. But she knew that as long as she could convince her users, she could still stand up again. She started publishing her designs on social media platforms and kept in touch with her clients, regularly offering discounts and pre-sales channels. Now, she has reopened her own clothing store and has become a fashion leader in the eyes of many customers.

In short, it is not difficult to promote and market your new business based on social media platforms, but it requires certain strategies and skills. The above suggestions, I hope to be helpful to the bankrupt who is looking for marketing channels.

Chapter 5: Career Planning and Restarting

Analyze career strengths and weaknesses and hobbies

Choosing the right career is crucial to rebuilding your life when you are broke. But how to find the right career? At this time, it is very necessary to help yourself make future career plans by analyzing your strengths and weaknesses and hobbies.

First, it is important to analyze your strengths and weaknesses. Advantages are their ability to show good ability and performance in the workplace. Advantages can include technical skills, language skills, interpersonal skills, management skills, etc. The bankrupt can look back at his or her previous work history and achievements and tap into his or her strengths. These advantages can be used as a basis for future career search, and can also be used as a verbal statement when applying for a job.

Secondly, it is also necessary to analyze your hobbies. Choosing a career that is related to your interests can increase your enthusiasm and participation in your work. It can also improve your happiness and job satisfaction. The bankrupt can review his life experience, analyze his interests and hobbies, and dig out the things and fields he really likes. In this regard, you can choose some interesting careers and find your own career direction.

Finally, you need to consider your future plans. According to their own strengths and weaknesses and hobbies, choose a suitable career direction, and have career development space and prospects. Bankruptcy can be based on their own advantages, choose their own familiar areas, or according to their own interests, in the new field of development. In addition, the employment situation and market demand need to be considered. Bankruptcies can learn about the current employment situation and job opportunities so that they can better choose a career that suits them.

In short, by analyzing their strengths and weaknesses and hobbies, you can help bankrupts find a career and future plan that suits them. When choosing a career, you also need to consider market demand and employment situation in order to better plan your career. I hope this article can help the bankrupt to choose the career direction.

Case:

Xiao Li is a young IT engineer who lost his stable job due to the bankruptcy of his former company. After a short period of disappointment, he decided to look for his own career again. He realized that he had a strong interest in game development, so he began to teach himself game development technology in his spare time. Eventually, he used his accumulated skills and experience to successfully enter an online game company to start his new career.

Mr. Wang, a bank clerk, had to give up his old job because of the pressure of debt when his former company went bankrupt. After careful consideration, he began to give full play to his management skills and interpersonal skills, into the personnel agency industry. After years of accumulation and hard work, he started an influential personnel agency and his life was back on track.

Ms. Zhang, a nurse at a public hospital, chose to continue her work after being laid off and joined a private hospital. She found that working in a private hospital not only had higher salary and more comfortable working environment, but also had more practical opportunities and more professional development space, which enabled her to find a satisfactory job again.

Mr. Li, a sales manager, chose to transition to e-commerce after his department was laid off. After a period of learning and adaptation, he became a sales maniac and achieved good results. With his professional experience, he gradually became a senior executive in the company and successfully re-established his career.

Xiao Wang is a young woman who used to work in hotel management. After her former company went bankrupt, she decided to learn new skills, self-taught and online courses to master marketing knowledge and skills, and eventually found a well-suited job at a well-known game company with better salary, benefits and career prospects.

Mr. Wang was an executive of an enterprise. He became an unemployed and bankrupt because the company went bankrupt due to poor management. Instead of being discouraged, Mr. Wang found his way from the strengths, weaknesses and interests of his chosen career. He had always loved music before, so he took advantage of this advantage to obtain a music teacher qualification certificate and became an excellent music teacher.

Ms. Zhao is a mother who quit her job to take care of her children and fell into debt on her husband's business road. After bankruptcy, Ms. Zhao took part in the training of an e-commerce company recommended by her friends and found herself particularly good at online marketing, so she devoted herself to the e-commerce field. With her efforts, her e-commerce business has flourished and got rid of debt.

Mr. Rowe is a retired soldier who went bankrupt due to personal problems. After bankruptcy, Mr. Luo chose to return to his profession and became a professional beekeeper. He gave full play to his professional experience and skills, established his own brand in the market, won the trust and respect of customers, and successfully got rid of debt.

Develop career goals and plans

In today's economic climate, many people may lose their jobs due to bankruptcy. However, this does not mean that the game is over. In fact, this is the perfect time to start reformulating your career goals and plans. With the following advice, the bankrupt can successfully restart his career and realize his dream.

Explore new, high-paying careers

Don't limit yourself to the industry you've been in. Dare to explore new, high-paying careers. This requires bankrupts to go beyond their comfort zone to learn and understand different industries and jobs. Even if it was a class that didn't seem to be related to his field, he could still try to understand it. There might be surprises. If your current abilities are not sufficient for your new career, make a study plan for yourself. Consider attending training courses, online learning or consulting professionals to improve your professional skills and knowledge. Getting a certificate or degree is also a good option.

Case:

Mr. Zhang worked as a carpenter in a furniture factory, but the factory went bankrupt because of market competition and poor management. Later, the unemployed Mr. Zhang decided to give up the unhealthy career of carpentry and try high-tech fields, learning programming and data analysis. Eventually, he managed to find a job at a technology company and constantly promoted himself to become a senior engineer at the company. With the high salary he earned from his job, he finally got out of debt.

Mr. Li used to work in the tourism industry, but because of the impact of the epidemic, the tourism market once fell into a trough, he had to go bankrupt. However, Mr. Li was not discouraged. Instead, he chose to learn about international trade and cross-border e-commerce. Through continuous learning and experimentation, Mr. Li successfully joined a cross-border e-commerce company and was promoted quickly, eventually helping him get rid of debt successfully.

Ms. Zhang used to be a salesperson, but because of market changes and fierce competition, she became one of the layoffs. However, Ms. Zhang did not lose confidence, she through learning and self-improvement, turned into the real estate intermediary industry. Through continuous communication and service, she has won the trust of customers and become the company's performance champion. With a high performance bonus, she finally managed to pay off her debt.

Mr. Li was originally a real estate developer, due to the industry downturn and poor management led to bankruptcy. He chose to transition into the internet industry and began learning programming and website design. Finally, he successfully joined a start-up company, through his unremitting efforts and innovative ideas, brought great business value and development opportunities for the company, and successfully walked out of the shadow of bankruptcy.

Mr. Zhang studied mechanical engineering in college and worked in an automation equipment company after graduation. However, as the company's market shrank, Mr. Zhang fell into debt after being laid off and worried about the future. He decided to learn Internet technology, successfully found a new job at an e-commerce company, and soon got a promotion and a raise, and paid off all his debts.

Ms. Wang, who previously worked in finance at the bank, suffered losses due to personal mistakes and owed a large amount of debt after being dismissed. Realizing that the education industry had a bright future, she began to study pedagogy and was hired by a kindergarten, and later became a manager of the kindergarten. Her income has also improved, and last year she paid off her debts.

Mr. Li, a salesman in the real estate industry, faced unemployment and debt as the industry became riskier. He thought of a career that would make him successful in a short time, and he was admitted to the police profession. His salary was not very high at first, but he worked hard to get the position of captain of the police force. Now he has worked for the police department for 10 years.

Mr. Liang used to work in production and management in a large automobile manufacturing company. He was laid off for various reasons in the company, which made him feel lost. But with a deep understanding of internet technology, he started a creative digital media company that quickly grew into a widely recognized company, earning huge revenues and paying off all debts.

Combine all your skills

Career development is not linear, but rather combinatorial. Make full use of all the skills you have mastered and combine them to see which jobs you can meet. In this way, you may discover that you have unique strengths and strengths, and your career path will be easier.

Case:

Xiao Wang, a former technology company's code farmer, was fired because of poor management. Instead of giving up, he taught himself programming, design and other skills and eventually joined a new Internet company as a product manager. Thanks to his quick thinking and excellent teamwork skills, the company quickly grew and Wang's position and salary increased.

Xiao Li, an unemployed salesman, was looking for a new job when he discovered an emerging market--online marketing. Through self-study and practice, he has become a professional network promoter, and his future prospects are very bright. Through hard work, he not only earned his living expenses, but also was able to pay off his previous debts.

Xiao Zhang, a former university lecturer, was forced to resign because of the college's budget shortfall. However, he didn't lose heart and turned to look for new job opportunities. Eventually, he was hired as a subject consultant at a large nursery, and through his teaching skills, the children got a better education and the nursery gained a better reputation and profits.

Xiao Chen is a former automotive engineer who lost his job due to the industry's decline. However, instead of being discouraged, he repositioned himself and turned to new opportunities. He discovered the fast-growing new energy vehicle industry and was welcomed by a start-up. He successfully transformed into an expert in new energy vehicles and played an important role in the company's R & D department.

Xiao Zhao is a former restaurant waiter who wants to try a new career. He found a new market-online education. He began using his restaurant experience to launch online cooking classes, which were widely welcomed. With his passion and skill, he became an elite in the online education industry and got out of the previous financial difficulties.

Go out of town to find a better job

Don't limit yourself to companies in your area of residence, and actively look for higher-paying and more promising positions in other places. Technology and transportation in this era make it easier to find work in other cities. Find job opportunities on social media to open up new horizons for career development.

Case:

Li Ming is the owner of a small clothing store. Business has been bad because of the fierce competition in the market. He eventually decided to close the shop, sell the inventory and go to the province to become an engineer. There, he received a higher salary and better benefits. Within a few months, he had successfully paid off all his debts and began planning to reopen a new store.

Wang Daming, a small supermarket owner, decided to go bankrupt and work as a tour guide in Yunnan because of fierce competition and profits that could not cope with high rents. There, he was praised for his work and paid well above his previous income. Soon after, he managed to pay off all his debts and used the accumulated funds to open a new small supermarket.

Liu Xiaogang is a private contractor whose business covers construction and renovation. Because of fierce competition from the same industry, there is less business and lower wages. Eventually, he had to go bankrupt and leave the industry, moving to Sichuan to work as a human resources executive. There, he was recognized by the company and given an important position. After a few months, he managed to pay off all his debts.

Zhang Xiaoning is a furniture designer whose business covers the entire domestic market. He faces financial hardship due to the high cost of living and other factors. After considering bankruptcy, he decided to move to Australia in search of better job opportunities. There, he received a good salary and high benefits. Soon after, he managed to pay off all his debts and opened his own studio locally.

Wu Xiaobo, an entrepreneur with his own small restaurant, began to lose business as new competitors entered. Eventually, he decided to go bankrupt and look for new business opportunities elsewhere. In Beijing, he found a high-paying job and his career quickly turned around. He managed to pay off all his debts and used the extra money to open a new local restaurant.

Become an expert in the industry

No matter what industry you are in, you should strive to become an expert in this industry. Make a practical plan, keep learning and keep abreast of the latest developments, so that you can step closer to becoming a leader in the industry.

Case:

Mr. Li, a construction engineer, lost his job when his previous company went bankrupt. Instead of giving up, he started his own hotel management business. Although inexperienced, he understands the market and competitors and is constantly expanding his skills by learning from current industry leaders. A few years later, his hotel chain was widely praised across the country, allowing him to pay off his debts.

Ms. Wang, a fashion designer, was in debt because of some business problems. However, she believed in her talent and creativity and started her own design studio. Her proficiency in different design software and fabrics, attention to detail and fashion trends, eventually gained widespread recognition and praise in the market, allowing her to return to the economic development track.

Mr. Cheung was an unemployed investment adviser who had faced financial crisis. He moved into education instead, exploring and learning on his own time to become a qualified English teacher. With his language skills and professional knowledge, he obtained a position as a university lecturer and successfully paid off his debts within the time limit.

Ms. Zhao, a former sales manager, was laid off by her company and faced financial pressure. Using her professional experience and violent communication skills, she founded a consulting firm that helps companies solve management challenges and marketing problems. Through summing up her own experience, building trust with customers and quick response, she successfully walked out of her financial quagmire one year later.

Mr. Xu runs his own wood processing plant and is struggling because of traffic conditions and procurement costs. He studied new production techniques and cost center of gravity analysis, repositioning his production line to save on material costs and energy use. His innovative approach provided better prices and quality to his customers, earned him higher profits, and managed to get out of debt within a few years.

Choose a position that enhances your abilities

Salary is not the only measure of a good job. We should put the ability improvement on a higher priority to make choices. Choosing a company that offers better learning and development opportunities and better meets your career goals and aspirations will be more beneficial than choosing a company with a higher salary but less room for development.

Case:

Mr. Zhao, an IT engineer, accepted a higher-paying position when he graduated, but found that the company's culture and prospects did not match his values. He decided to resign, and as his professional skills and abilities continued to improve, he soon found a position that was more suitable for him and his salary increased several times.

Mr. Zhang, an engineer in his forties, owed a lot of debt because his factory went bankrupt and lost his job. Despite his years of work experience, he couldn't find a job with a higher salary because of his age and education. Later, he took the advice of a friend and gave up a higher-paying job in favor of a lower-paying position with more room for development. With his hard work and professionalism, he quickly gained recognition from his superiors and was promoted. A few years later, he moved to a bigger company, doubled his salary several times, and finally paid off his debts and got out of the debt mire.

Ms. Wang is a newly graduated college student, family economic conditions are not very good, need to support themselves. She joined a small company as a clerk. Although the salary was not high, her job was easy and stable, giving her time and energy to further improve her ability. She works hard every day, studies diligently, and constantly improves her work quality and professional skills through self-study and training. As time went on, her ability was gradually recognized by her boss, and she was promoted and received a higher salary. Eventually, she became popular in the industry and became a successful professional woman.

Ms. Zhang is a driving school coach working in a small driving school. Because of the fierce competition in the coaching industry, her salary is not high and she can barely make ends meet every month. She felt that she needed to further improve her abilities and skills before she could have a place in the industry. As a result, she continued to improve her driving skills and coaching skills through training and self-study. With her professional qualities and hard work, she successfully obtained the senior coach qualification certificate, and obtained a higher salary and broader development opportunities in a large driving school.

Mr. Li is an equipment operation and maintenance engineer who has been working in a small IT company. Mr. Li lost his job because of financial problems in the company. He felt confused and confused, but he didn't give up. He knew that if he wanted to stand up again, he had to rely on his courage and ability to make a new journey. Through self-study and training, he constantly improved his technical level and professionalism, and finally got a job in a large Internet company. Although the salary at the beginning is not high, Mr. Li is confident about his future. He believes that with his ability, he will be able to get better career development and higher salary.

Mr. Wang is a construction worker who works for a small construction company. Because the company is relatively small, Mr. Wang's salary is not high, it is difficult to maintain the normal expenses of the family. However, he did not give up. He uses his spare time to continuously improve his work skills and professional accomplishment through self-study and training. Slowly, his ability was recognized by his superiors and colleagues, and he received more opportunities and higher salaries. Eventually, he successfully embarked on a path of professional success, becoming an excellent architect and starting his own engineering company.

In short, redefining career goals and plans is a process that requires self-experimentation, continuous learning, and never giving up. Through the above suggestions, I hope to provide some help and confidence for those affected by bankruptcy to move towards a new starting point in their careers.

Develop relationships and sell yourself

For people who are already broke, finding a job they want again is not only a financial need, but also a psychological one. But how do you stand out in a competitive workplace? This requires us to develop relationships, sell ourselves, and get the position we want. Below I will give suggestions from several aspects.

Develop self-confidence

Self-confidence is the foundation of success, bankruptcy does not mean that you have no ability, but a temporary failure. So we need to give ourselves encouragement and confidence that we can do the job. At the same time, if we use our language and body language properly, we can make people feel confident.

Case:

Mr. Zhang is the boss of a small company, but his company is going bankrupt because of the fierce competition in the market. Faced with this situation, Mr. Zhang felt very depressed and lost, but he decided to cheer up. He began to develop his self-confidence and actively looked for job opportunities. Finally, he found a stable job in a large company, and he succeeded in getting out of bankruptcy by his own efforts and persistence.

Ms. Wang used to run a small clothing store, but because of high procurement costs and declining sales, the store began to go bankrupt. In the face of this situation, Ms. Wang felt desperate and helpless. But as time went on, she came to realize that she had to pull herself together and look for new opportunities. Ms. Wang began to grow herself, such as learning sales skills and interpersonal skills, and eventually she successfully found a sales job and was back on the road to development.

Mr. Li is a trader whose company has turned from profit to loss due to market volatility and rising procurement costs. Soon, Mr. Li was in financial trouble. In this dilemma, Mr. Li felt weak and lost, but later, he decided to summon up courage, find a solution, and pick himself up. He learned how to resolve debt, look for investment and market opportunities, and eventually successfully get out of debt.

Mr. Ma is a freelancer, but his financial situation is becoming increasingly precarious due to unstable income and rising expenses. In this situation, Mr. Ma decided to take action and began to learn how to manage money and make money. He gradually increased his self-confidence and began to face difficulties more positively. Later, he succeeded in finding a stable job and worked his way out of financial difficulties with his own goals and plans.

Ms. Zhang used to be a salesman, but her salary could not meet her living expenses. In order to increase her income, she began to learn new skills and cultivate emerging businesses in her free time. As time went on, she gradually found that her strength and ability had been improved and she successfully started a business of her own. Ms. Zhang, who regained her self-confidence, not only walked out of the predicament, but also created new wealth and opportunities.

Mr. Zhang is a businessman who has just gone bankrupt, losing all his assets and the trust of his borrowers. However, he did not give up, but devoted himself to learning and improving his abilities. Eventually, he managed to get back on his feet by building a small company, realizing his self-worth and financial independence.

As a result, Ms. Li's former company went bankrupt, carrying huge debts and negative lawsuits, and was under pressure from public opinion in the society. But instead of being dejected, she worked hard to get out of debt by actively pursuing education and improving her personal abilities, eventually getting a new high-paying job.

Mr. Wang is also a businessman, he once because of business mistakes and bankruptcy, into the plight of unemployment and poverty. However, he did not give up, but through his unremitting efforts and continuous learning, he learned new business experience and knowledge, and finally successfully re-founded a company, realizing personal and economic rebirth.

Ms. Yang was in trouble because of the bankruptcy of her company. She once lived on the streets and lost her confidence and courage in life. However, with the encouragement of her family and friends, she gradually regained her self-confidence and laid a new career foundation for herself through various trainings and studies. Eventually, she got a new job, which helped her out of poverty and unemployment.

Mr. Li ran a small factory, but his business was hit hard by the recession and the pressure of market competition, and the company went bankrupt. However, he did not give up, but by going abroad to study and study related technologies, he gained new professional abilities and eventually started a new company again, regaining economic success and glory.

Learn to communicate with people

Communication is the key to career opportunities and successful relationships. We should be good at listening, reflecting the importance and concern of others, and thinking from each other's point of view. After each session, reflect on yourself and record your own shortcomings and improvements in communication.

Case:

Mr. Li used to be a successful entrepreneur, but his company finally went bankrupt due to mismanagement and fierce market competition. Having lost his career, he was deeply in debt. However, in the communication with creditors, he gradually learned to understand each other's difficulties, they began to communicate with each other sincerely. In the end, Mr. Li won the trust of his creditors and was given the opportunity to reduce his debt. He also took the opportunity to reflect on his own shortcomings and re-planned his life and career. Eventually, he became a successful entrepreneur, and Mr. Li found his value.

Xiao Wang is an unemployed person, he because of make a living, went to the bar to collect feelings. One day, he met a big boss here, and he talked to him. However, it was clear that Xiao Wang's experience had not been bright in the past, and the big boss did not think much of him. However, Wang did not give up, he began to try to understand each other's ideas, and the big boss's needs interface docking, explore their own advantages and continuous supplementary learning, finally got the big boss's favor, overall took over a small company. Xiao Wang worked hard to get out of the quagmire and predicament of poverty and unemployment, mastered the time, got out of the haze of society through interpersonal communication, and became a successful entrepreneur.

Xiao Liu is a professional manager. He used to work in a large enterprise. However, due to his lack of personal attainments and poor performance, he was laid off by the company. He faced unemployment and credit card debt. However, Xiao Liu did not give up. He began to improve himself constantly, enhance his competitiveness, master more knowledge and skills through study, and finally got a high-paying position in a new company. Xiao Liu started again and became an excellent manager. He also felt the beauty of life in the new challenge and ushered in the turning point of life.

Ms. Zhang once opened a small jewelry store, but she had to close because of the bad market. This made her feel very lost and began to face debts that could not be repaid. But she didn't give up. She learned to communicate actively with her creditors, identify her business problems, and reopened an online store shortly after closing, doing well in new areas, far exceeding her expected earnings. Ms. Zhang's personal charm and professional habits attract more customers 'support. She also realizes that in terms of innovation, entrepreneurship and operation, she must improve her professional skills and accomplishment in order to survive in the highly competitive market.

Mr. Wang is a designer, but his work is often criticized, misunderstood, he left the design industry disheartened. Recently, a recruitment from a company has rekindled his passion for design. During the interview, Mr. Wang deeply reflected on the technical skills and achievements of the post. He always insisted on improving his skills and abilities and always kept a modest and serious attitude. This was appreciated by the top management of the company, and eventually Mr. Wang got the position and became the leader in the industry. Mr. Wang's journey has become an example and inspiration for many other peers, and also warns us to always stand on the position of the winner, learn and master advanced skills, become an expert in life and succeed in this new era.

Build a Social networks

Make an effort to build your own Social networks. Socialize actively by attending industry conferences, social events nearby, volunteering, and more. The purpose of networking is not to get a job by simply using relationships, but to get more good opportunities through good relationships.

Case:

Mr. Zhang used to be an entrepreneur, but for various reasons, his company finally went bankrupt, with debts as high as 1 million yuan. But Mr. Zhang doesn't give up. He actively participates in industry conferences and social events, communicates with people in different fields and looks for opportunities. Eventually, he rebuilt his career as a product manager at a startup through a friend he met at a social event.

Ms. Li used to be a housewife, but her husband suddenly lost his job and the family was in financial trouble. To help her family through difficult times, she actively participates in local volunteer activities and builds friendships with like-minded volunteers. At one such event, she befriended a project manager from a large company and eventually got a job in marketing through him to pick up her career.

Mr. Wang used to be the owner of a small business, but the company has been losing money because of fierce market competition. Eventually, the company went bankrupt and he was heavily in debt. In this case, Mr. Wang met some senior industry insiders by attending various industry conferences and social events, and asked them for help and advice. With these resources and his own experience, Mr. Wang successfully entered the senior management team of another company and created a new profit growth point.

Ms. Zhang used to be a senior sales consultant, but she had to leave her job because of the company's business difficulties. Since then, she has been active in industry exhibitions and networking events and has established a number of industry relationships. Soon after, through those connections, she landed a job at a new Internet company, rekindling her professional passion.

Mr. Guo was a senior executive, but he was forced to leave his position when the company was in trouble. He found that his resume and experience did not help him find a suitable job again. As a result, he began to participate in various volunteer and charity activities, and gradually met many influential people through these activities. He used those connections to land an executive position at an emerging fintech company, which allowed him to regain his career.

Mr. Li is a bankrupt entrepreneur. He once ran a large company, but because of poor management, the company went bankrupt and was in debt. However, Mr. Li did not give up. He actively participated in industry conferences and summits, met many industry insiders and experts in these activities, and got many valuable suggestions. At the same time, he joined a volunteer organization to contribute to the community through his own strength. In the end, Mr. Li found a good job again through his own efforts and social activities, and got out of debt.

Ms. Wang was a person who once opened a small shop, but went bankrupt because of the increased debt pressure caused by poor management of the store. Undeterred, however, Ms. Wang socialized and joined a local business organization, where she met like-minded people and got some business advice and opportunities. In the end, Ms. Wang regained her confidence through her own efforts and social activities, found a good job again and got out of debt.

Mr. Zhang is an unemployed middle-aged man who has to borrow money to get by because of his family's financial difficulties. But because of his lack of social interaction, he could not find a suitable job. However, in a community activity, Mr. Zhang met many volunteers and people from all walks of life and made some new friends. These new friends constantly introduced him to job opportunities and gave him a lot of experience and advice. Eventually, Mr. Zhang found a good job through the introduction and recommendation of friends, and got out of the debt quagmire.

Ms. Yang is a housewife. She has to borrow money to support her family because of the excessive expenses. However, Ms. Yang did not give up. She made some new friends by attending various social activities, including friends 'parties, weddings and so on. These new friends gave her a lot of experience and advice, and also helped her find some opportunities for family subsidies. Eventually, Ms. Yang found a good domestic job and got out of debt.

Mr. Xu is a university graduate who cannot find a suitable job and is forced to borrow money to make ends meet. However, Mr. Xu did not give up. He made many professionals and scholars by attending various social activities and academic conferences. These new friends gave him a lot of advice on employment and career planning, and also provided him with some suitable job opportunities. Eventually, Mr. Xu found an ideal job with their help and got out of debt.

Recognize your strengths and weaknesses

Recognize your strengths and weaknesses. Identify your strengths and weaknesses so that you can make the most of your strengths and avoid loopholes in your weaknesses. Get constant feedback and evaluation to keep your self-evaluation objective. Not all of us are omnipotent, so we need to play different roles in the team so that the team can better collaborate and innovate.

Case:

Mr. Zhang used to run a small kitchen supply store, but he eventually went bankrupt due to poor management and a shrinking market. After a period of shock and self-reflection, he realized he had great sales and communication skills. So he decided to apply for a job as a salesman in a large supermarket chain. He showed off his strengths during the interview and admitted that he wasn't very good at finance. In the end, he succeeded in getting the job and continued to develop his strengths in his work, gradually stepping out of the shadow of bankruptcy.

Ms. Wang used to be the treasurer of a small business, but she lost her job and incurred a lot of debt because the company's capital chain broke. After a painful experience, she decided to re-examine her strengths and weaknesses. She found herself very careful and organized in her work, but weak in marketing and business development. So she decided to stop focusing on financial management and instead focus on sales. She looked for sales positions with different companies and successfully landed her new job with a large pharmaceutical company. She has brought her carefulness and organization into full play and has made great progress in her sales skills.

Mr. Li is a young professional photographer who used to start his own business, but he had to give up his business because of the difficult completion of the project and the sluggish market. He was keenly aware that he had great skills and creativity in photography, but lacked experience in business and negotiation. In order to change his career, he began taking classes to learn business skills and actively contacted different photography jobs. In an interview with an advertising agency, he showed off his excellent photography skills. Despite his shortcomings in business, he has made significant progress and finally succeeded in getting the job.

Ms. Zhang used to be a freelance translator, but she couldn't make a living because of the fierce competition in the market. Reflecting on her experience, she found that her native language was excellent and that there was much room for improvement in public speaking and communication. So she started looking for language-related work and eventually found an opportunity to work for a multinational company. In the interview, she fully demonstrated her language talent, although there are still deficiencies in communication skills, but she participated in the company's training classes, and constantly improve their skills, and finally found a new stable job.

Mr. Cheng used to be a programmer, but because the project failed, he lost his job and faced huge debts. He believes in his excellent programming skills, but he lacks a lot in teamwork and project management. He began learning skills related to collaboration and communication and looking for new programming projects. Eventually, he found his dream job at an internet company, demonstrated his excellent programming skills and improved teamwork and communication skills, and finally managed to get out of debt.

Xiao Wang went bankrupt because of his investment failure, but he didn't give up on himself. He realized that he had a strong verbal ability and decided to go into sales. He used his strengths to build good relationships with customers through effective communication and successfully found a high-paying sales job.

After Mr. Zhang's company went bankrupt, he was stuck in a huge debt. However, in the process of self-examination, he found that he was very good at processing complex information, so he began to develop into the financial field. Through in-depth study of the market and prudent investment strategy, he got out of trouble in a short time.

Ms. Liu went bankrupt because of her personal investment mistakes, but she did not lose confidence. She decided to switch to a relatively stable industry and applied for a job in the insurance industry. After a period of training and practice, she found herself adept at building trust and empathy with clients and successfully emerged in the insurance industry.

Mr. Li is going to be a sales agent after his business failed and he is in debt for millions. In the process of learning, he found that he was not good at finding new customers, but he knew how to maintain existing customers. As a result, he learned from his colleagues how to skillfully respond to customers 'needs, and used his eloquence and emotional intelligence to sign a large number of orders, and finally succeeded in getting out of debt.

Ms. Wang, whose company went bankrupt during the recession, realized she had a gift for marketing and brand management. So she moved to another company as a marketing manager. She has managed to get out of debt by understanding the market and consumers and effectively promoting the company's brand and products.

Keep learning and growing

Fifth, keep learning. In a competitive workplace, knowledge and skills change rapidly. Having a good career plan can help us keep learning in this field and keep ourselves up to date. At the same time, actively use Internet resources, as well as looking for scientific and technological achievements and innovative practices, and strive to cultivate their own innovation and competitiveness.

Case:

Xiao Liu is a young man who has just gone bankrupt. He lost all his assets and possessions, was unable to find a job, and was in trouble. But he didn't give up. He kept learning and used Internet resources to learn new skills, such as data analysis and artificial intelligence. Eventually, he found a high-paying job as a data analyst and managed to get out of poverty.

Xiao Wang was a young IT engineer who went bankrupt because of his mistakes. He felt very guilty and lost, but he did not give up. He actively sought out innovations and technological achievements and used the Internet to build his own company. Through his own innovative practice, he finally succeeded in getting out of the debt quagmire.

Mr. Zhang is a middle-aged man who lost all his fortune because of his failure in the stock market. But he didn't give up, and he began to learn how to use the Internet and e-commerce platforms to start a business. Through his own efforts, he built his own e-commerce platform on the Internet and used social media and Internet advertising to promote his business. In the end, he beat the debt and re-rooted in the wave of the Internet economy.

Miss Gao is a young designer. Her company went bankrupt due to business reasons. But she didn't give up, and she began to learn how to innovate and use the company's remaining resources. Eventually, she managed to create her own brand through digital design and innovation, successfully repositioning herself in the high-end fashion market.

Mr. Li, a middle-aged man, went bankrupt because he lost money in business. But he didn't give up, he actively looked for other jobs. He successfully switched to become a business developer for an Internet company and played an important role in the company's business development and marketing. In the end, he managed to get out of debt and rebuild a new beginning for himself and his family.

Mr. Zhang is a former entrepreneur who went bankrupt because of poor management. Undaunted, he used the internet to learn new skills and knowledge, eventually becoming a professional internet marketer and earning enough money to pay off all his debts.

Xiao Li is an unemployed person, because of the family's economic pressure, in the friend's recommendation, she began to learn Internet marketing. With his diligence and hard work, Xiao Li became an excellent e-commerce seller and finally made enough money on the Internet to get out of the financial crisis.

Lao Wang used to be an unemployed person. In order to earn money, he once managed his business, but in the case of poor management, he was deeply in debt. However, after joining an Internet company, Lao Wang under high pressure, but also constantly learning, practice, finally ushered in the career reversal, successfully paid off all debts, to achieve a new height in life.

Xiao Liu is an aspiring young man who has entered the quagmire of business because of poor management and is troubled by a series of debts. However, through his own hard work, he kept his confidence and did not give up, found his own "treasure" from the Internet, started a brand-new career, and got rid of all debts.

For the young Xiao Zhang, he suffered from academic failure and financial crisis, but with his unremitting efforts and continuous learning, he found his favorite career and development direction, successfully found a good job, and regained a new starting point for his life and career.

Publicize one's merits

Promote yourself by promoting your strengths in various ways. Through the use of personal websites, personal blogs, Social networks, and related professional media, communicate their ideas and experiences and the characteristics of goods or services, so that they or their products can be better known and recognized by potential customers or recruiters.

Case:

Mr. Wang is a bankrupt small-business owner. He made some operational mistakes carelessly, which led to the break of the company's capital chain and eventually bankruptcy. Mr. Wang did not give up because of this. After a period of thinking and summing up, he decided to share his experience and lessons with other entrepreneurs. He has created his own personal blog on the Internet and updates it frequently, and has also established his own personal brand on Social networks to continuously promote himself and his experience. Soon after, Mr. Wang was poached by a foreign-funded company and became one of their executives.

Ms. Zhang is an employee who lost her job because of the downsizing of the company. She quickly discovered that in this day and age, having some networking skills is crucial. So ms. zhang taught herself computer programming, built her own website using wordpress, and wrote about her previous work experience and skills. She also posts some skill sharing on Social networks and is active in the tech community. With continuous learning and hard work, Ms. Zhang got the attention of an international software company and finally got a high-paying technical job.

Mr. Li was once a senior executive at a large company, but was eventually fired because of poor performance and management problems. Unwilling to waste his overwhelming experience and resources, Mr. Li began his own personal consulting work in online media. He offers unique services ranging from public company positions to corporate restructurings, as well as communicating his ideas and methods to a wider audience through online media and public speaking. Soon after, he received consulting offers from several companies to become a consultant in feasibility analysis and corporate strategic planning.

Ms. Luo is a beauty and fashion person who lost her job because of the changing times. Deep down, she always wanted to execute her dream of becoming a fashion consultant. So she set up her own personal web page on loft to tell her thoughts and experiences. Ms. Luo also actively cooperates with fashion bloggers to provide professional fashion advice and clothing brand recommendations for consumers. Soon, Ms. Luo received an invitation from a fashion magazine to become a fashion article writer with high social visibility and credibility.

Mr. Liu is a bankrupt foreign trade service provider, which is facing operational difficulties due to the cold market and fierce competition. After a period of reflection and reflection, he decided to use the power of the internet to expand his business and publish information on repair services and inventory on social media and professional foreign trade forums. Although few people paid attention to his information at first, with continuous efforts, he was always able to find customers who were willing to cooperate with him. Eventually, Mr. Liu re-established his own trade service company and became a large-scale foreign trade company.

Mr. Zhang used to be the sales director of a large enterprise. Due to poor management of the company, he eventually went bankrupt. He started his own personal branding when he was unemployed, showcasing his expertise and experience through Social networks and personal websites. Eventually, he landed an enthusiastic job at a small and medium-sized company and became the company's senior vice president of sales.

Xiaowen used to be an administrative assistant in a large company. She lost her source of income because of layoffs. She began posting her work experience and skills, as well as her hobbies and life insights, on her personal blog and social media. Eventually, she landed a job as a brand promotion manager for an emerging internet company.

Mr. Yang is a freelancer whose main job is to write market research reports for a small company, but as the company's business shrinks, he has lost a long-term stable source of income. His solution is to promote his professional skills and work experience through Social networks and personal websites. Eventually, he was tapped by a large corporation and became their consultant.

Kobayashi, a former garment factory worker, lost her job when the factory stopped operating. She began promoting her personal brand by displaying her sewing skills and designs on Social networks and personal blogs. Eventually, she became a partner to many fashion designers, becoming one of their main suppliers.

Mr. Zhang used to be a senior engineer in an IT company, but he was forced to lose his job because of the company's poor management. He began showcasing his technical skills and experience, as well as his personal projects and research, on his personal blog and social media. Eventually, he became a partner and chief technology officer of a technology innovation company.

Win people's trust

We need to build a foundation of trust in our relationships and sales. Focus on letting others know our talents and ideas, helping others solve problems, and helping them achieve their goals. And when appropriate, look for opportunities to help others and make them feel valued.

Case:

Xiao Li is the boss of a private enterprise. Due to poor management, the bankruptcy of the enterprise leads to poverty. But he didn't give up his passion for helping others. He often volunteers for people in the community, helping students with homework and so on. In the community, he impressed many neighbors and students with his generous and helpful image, gradually winning everyone's trust and respect. Eventually, because of this helpful spirit, he was chosen by the hiring manager of a large company and successfully entered the company as a senior position, receiving a good salary.

Xiao Zhang, a college graduate, encountered many difficulties in finding a job, which led to his low state of mind, loss and frustration. However, he did not give up and continued to look for entrepreneurial opportunities. In the process, he often provides business consulting to others, helping entrepreneurs improve their business plans and improve their business capabilities. In this way, he demonstrated his talent and professionalism, earned people's trust and respect, and finally gained a high-paying job opportunity.

Xiao Wang is a young accountant who works in a small company. As the company's business has been stagnant, leading to the company's financial situation from bad to worse, and eventually bankruptcy. However, Xiao Wang did not give up. He used his professional knowledge and skills to help some small businesses standardize their financial management processes and improve their financial situation. His skills and sense of responsibility have been well received in the industry, allowing him to be favored by a large enterprise and successfully achieve career transformation.

Xiao Chen is a young designer who had previously led his company to collapse for personal reasons. However, he did not despair, but through the cooperation with other designers, let himself get a lot of opportunities to show and develop. He excels in design and has always been at the forefront of innovation. As a result, he gained recognition from many clients and was eventually recruited by a well-known advertising agency as a senior designer with a competitive salary.

Xiao Xie is a sales manager with 20 years of experience. However, due to poor management of the company, it was in trouble after being laid off.

Instead of giving up, he developed his own sales solutions by understanding the research industry market and trying to sell as a company. In the sales process, he gave customers better choices and better experiences, and won praise from many industry leaders at some trade shows. After gaining their trust, he was successfully recruited by a large multinational company and became a senior sales manager of the company, receiving a better salary.

Xiao Wang used to be an executive in a company. However, due to some management problems, he was fired, leaving him bankrupt. Later, he began to allocate some time to help his friends in the market, and became an independent consultant to provide professional assistance. Because of his expertise and innovative salesmanship, his consulting business grew and people began to praise him. His professional and professional abilities were recognized, so some companies began to pay attention to him and invited him to join their teams.

Xiao Liu is an engineer who has just been bankrupted from a technology company. He quickly saw a realisation opportunity to turn his skills into business and began volunteering in the community to assist with various projects, particularly technical support for small and medium-sized businesses. Over time, Xiao Liu was noticed by many enterprises that needed technical support, and his expertise was widely recognized. He gradually turned into a senior engineer and gained better career opportunities in the international market.

In general, developing self-confidence, learning to communicate with others, building your own Social networks, recognizing your strengths and weaknesses, learning and growing, promoting yourself and selling yourself in various ways, and winning people's trust are all important methods and suggestions for expanding interpersonal relationships, selling yourself, and getting the position you want. Only constant efforts can lead us to success.

Chapter 6: Dealing with family and social interaction

Family support and arrangements

When people are in a state of bankruptcy, their self-esteem and confidence often take a hit, and they often need to seek support. Here are some useful tips to help those who are in a state of bankruptcy seek support in their families and reorient themselves.

Be honest with family members

When people face bankruptcy, they often feel afraid or ashamed, but the truth is. Sharing your situation with your family and seeking their support and encouragement can build trust and send a positive message.

Case:

Mr. Zhang was an entrepreneur whose mismanagement of his business led to the bankruptcy of his company. Faced with a debt situation, he did not hesitate to find his family and confess his situation to them. With the support and help of his family, he started again, re-started his business, and finally succeeded in achieving a full turnaround.

Ms. Li was a young investor who took a chance on a new business, but unfortunately it went bankrupt. Feeling at a loss, she told her family what had happened to her. Her family provided her with timely help, allowing her to move on and restart her investment path.

Mr. Wang was an over-spender who spent all his savings in just a few years, leading to personal bankruptcy. In order to solve his dilemma, he embarked on a path of honesty. He told his family that he had no savings and needed their help to support himself. The warm hugs and support of his family helped him pick himself up and become a man again.

Ms. Zhang is a young self-media person, her video channel has received a lot of attention and praise. But because of her too radical speech, leading to the critical moment advertisers have withdrawn, so that her future cast a shadow. In the face of her predicament, she could not bear it alone, she embarked on a path of sincerity and love. She confessed her situation to her family, who understood and supported her in restarting her career.

Mr. Liu is an unfortunate worker whose factory went bankrupt. Because he had his family with him, he didn't choose the easy equipment. He was carrying a heavy burden and could only solve his predicament by telling his family. His family gave him imagination and help on top of it, allowing him to find his own direction and restart the process of re-hopping.

Mr. Zhang is a young entrepreneur. He once owned a company that made a lot of money but went bankrupt because of lack of funds due to poor management. Facing the reality of bankruptcy, Mr. Zhang chose to be honest, apologize to his family and ask for their support and understanding. After a period of family consultation and support, Mr. Zhang finally came back, rebuilt his business and earned more wealth.

Ms. Wang is a middle-aged woman who has fallen into debt because of a failed investment. In order to get more money and avoid losing her home, Ms. Wang apologized to her family and confessed her situation, and asked her family to help her through the difficulties. Thankfully, Ms. Wang's family was very supportive and gave her generous help when she needed it most, allowing her to get back on her feet and get back on the road to hard work.

Mr. Li is a young man who failed in his entrepreneurial endeavors when he tried to start his own company due to lack of experience and resources. Mr. Li confessed his plight to his family and asked for their support and understanding. Mr. Li's family gave him firm support and encouragement, and he finally made a successful comeback and achieved more achievements and wealth.

Ms. Liu, a young woman studying abroad, was in dire straits when she returned to China after failing to invest and leaving her in debt. At first, Ms. Liu chose to hide her family, but later she mustered up the courage to confess her situation to her family and ask for help. Ms. Liu's family was very supportive, providing her with financial and moral support to brave and get through the most difficult moments.

Mr. Zhao is a retired old man who made a mistake in investing in stocks, resulting in his pension not enough to support his daily life. Mr. Zhao told his family the sad news, and the family eased his burden and mental stress, helped him re-plan his life and financial strategy, and gave him practical help when he needed it, so that he could get through the most difficult period.

Mr. Li, the owner of a small company, suffered from severe depression after an investment mistake left the company in debt of millions of yuan. Finally, with the support and encouragement of his family, he openly confessed his predicament to his family and received financial support from his brothers and sisters to successfully overcome the difficulties.

Ms. Chen is an unemployed single mother, the child is still in high school, the family financial constraints, has owed hundreds of thousands of yuan in debt. In the face of difficulties, she resolutely decided to confess her situation with her parents, got the support and encouragement of her parents, worked out a debt relief plan together, and finally successfully repaid the debt and lived a happy family life.

Mr. Wang, a retired old man with limited annual income, unfortunately fell ill. However, due to insufficient medical insurance and high medical expenses, the family's life is difficult financially. Later, he had frank and supportive communication with his family and received financial support and help from his children. Eventually, he recovered and his family returned to a stable life.

Xiao Liu is a young designer who failed to start a business, losing money and being heavily in debt. In the face of this situation, he confessed his experience to his family, got the support and encouragement of his family, and provided him with warm and warm family care. Xiao Liu first put his focus on the family, then rely on the help of his family to gradually struggle, and finally in the family support to re-start a successful business.

Discuss financial plans with family members

Talk to family members about financial planning to help you recover during the recovery process. Family members can help you with budget planning or job hunting, which can help restore your confidence. Also, talking about the financial planning process can help family members better understand your situation and support your recovery plan.

Case:

Xiao Wang was the boss of a small company, but the company finally went bankrupt because of the shrinking market and poor management. Xiao Wang is both resistant and frustrated. He feels that financial management has failed. But with the help of his wife and parents, he calmly analyzed his debt, worked out a repayment plan and turned to his family for help. His family was very supportive and came together to make plans to dutifully put their savings together to pay off the debt. Finally, Xiao Wang managed to get rid of debt and start a new life.

Xiao Zhang is a young white-collar worker, but after his family paid high medical expenses and some living expenses, his credit card debt increased rapidly and finally got into trouble. He was desperate, but his parents and siblings were supportive, working together to develop a repayment plan and teaching him how to save money and manage his finances. His family not only arranged for him to collect money, but also helped him find a higher-paying job, and finally Xiao Zhang managed to get out of debt.

Xiao Liu, a young migrant worker, is feeling depressed and depressed as his debts soar due to job instability and delayed wages. He has no other family, but a friend who relies on a support group supports him in making monthly plans and stabilizing his income. More importantly, they helped him upgrade his skills and increase his income. After the debt was paid off, Liu joined the group to help others with their financial problems.

Xiao Li is a middle-aged man who used to make a lot of money, but his excessive consumption and bad investment led to his bankruptcy. He felt that fate was unfair and that there was no hope for him. But encouraged by his family, he decided to examine himself, discuss one-on-one with his family and work out a repayment plan. With the support of his family, he began to pay attention to his expenses, repay his debts seriously and responsibly, and finally succeeded in getting out of debt.

Xiao Chen is a college student who has fallen into huge debt due to his parents 'illness and tuition payments. He felt so desperate that he even considered dropping out of school and giving up his future. But with the help of classmates, teachers and family, he worked out a detailed repayment plan and added his own learning aids to save money. His family gave him unlimited help and support, and he eventually managed to get out of debt by paying back intermittently.

Mr. Zhang is an entrepreneur working in the real estate industry, but his company suddenly faces a huge debt crisis, and he owes a lot of debt and cannot repay it. In consultation with his family, he decided to mortgage his property to pay off his debts as soon as possible. Through the joint efforts of the whole family, his company has regained its stability and achieved new development opportunities.

Ms. Li's husband, an engineer working in the mining industry, suddenly went into debt because of changes in the market environment and poor management. In a joint discussion with her family, Ms. Li proposed to invest her family's savings in her husband's company to help her get out of debt crisis. Eventually, they successfully completed the repayment and gradually recovered from their unfavorable financial situation.

Mr. Wang was an insurance broker working in the insurance industry, but his company lost a lot of assets due to negligence, which led to mistakes in the company's operation and increased claims, forcing him into debt crisis. In consultation with his family, Mr. Wang decided to invest his shares and bonuses in the company into repayment. Eventually, he made the payments and regained financial stability.

Ms. Liu is a sales manager working in the electronics industry, but due to market changes and poor management of the company, her company suddenly went bankrupt, leaving her facing financial crisis. After discussions with her family, Ms. Liu decided not to sell her home, but to inject her private assets into the company to repay the loan. Eventually, she managed to get out of financial trouble.

Mr. Zhao is an entrepreneur in the tourism industry, but due to operational mistakes, his company suddenly fell into bankruptcy crisis at the end of 2018. With the full support of his family members, he decided to inject the family's savings and other assets into the company in order to successfully repay the debt. Eventually, his company returned to normal operation step by step and achieved redevelopment.

Reposition yourself in the family

If you have lost your job or are in a bad financial situation, consider temporarily taking on other roles in the family, such as doing housework, taking care of children's education, buying food, etc. At the same time, seek help from family members, both physically and psychologically.

Case:

Mr. Li is a bankrupt purchasing agent. He returned home after going bankrupt as a result of the outbreak. Starting a new life, he took on the responsibility of housework and children's education. He realizes that family is the most important thing and does his best to take care of and accompany his family every day. His wife, impressed by his devotion to the family, worked harder and the family gradually got out of debt.

Ms. Wang used to be a conductor, but she had to resign to take care of her family because of the heavy burden on her family. Soon after, the husband who failed in business also returned home. Ms. Wang decided to take on all the housework and let her husband relax at home or go out to find a job. She also began to teach herself crafts and began making handmade products to sell online to help her family earn a certain income. In this way, the family gradually out of economic difficulties.

Mr. Zhang used to be an entrepreneur, but he went bankrupt because of the risk of doing business. Although he was very sad, he decided to go home and take care of his wife and children. His excellent work at home and with the children allowed his wife to devote herself to her work outside the home. Because of his psychological support and the family's efforts, the family's financial situation soon improved.

Ms. Zhao used to be a teacher, but because her child was ill, she had to quit her job to take care of the child at home. This leads to family financial difficulties. Knowing this, the husband resigned and returned home to take responsibility for housework and children's education. Ms. Zhao is very touched and tries her best to take care of her children and family. Thanks to her husband's support and encouragement, she returned to education and the family gradually got out of debt.

Mr. Li decided to return to his hometown to live with his parents after failing to start a business, accumulating debts and finding it difficult to pay for renting a house. At home, he did housework every day, took care of children and the elderly, and actively looked for job opportunities, and finally found a stable job in a small business. Through self-reliance, he finally got out of debt and restored his family to a happy life.

After her husband lost his job, Ms. Wang's family faced heavy financial pressure. Her mother was seriously ill and needed care, and her daughter was still at school. She decided to dismiss the servant, do her own housework, take charge of the children's education, grow vegetables at home, and use the rest of the money to pay off her debts. Through persistent efforts, she eventually paid off all her debts, regained her confidence and created a better future for her family.

Mr. Zhang's pursuit of his dream of starting a business failed, he lost all his investments, but also burdened with huge debts. With his wife's support and encouragement, he decided to retire first and devote himself to being a househusband. He is responsible for housework, accompanying children, and letting his wife focus on work outside to earn more income. After a year of hard work, he not only helped his wife share the pressure, but also enabled the family to achieve financial freedom.

After her husband went bankrupt, Ms. Lu faced a severe financial crisis, but she didn't give up. To support her family, she decided to be a full-time housewife. She guards the family day and night, is responsible for the children's study and life, but also shares part of her husband's work, making an important contribution to the family's financial situation. In the end, her efforts paid off, and the marriage and family came back to life.

After losing his job, Mr. Lu fell into a debt crisis. His family members worked like crazy, but they still couldn't repay the debt. Mr. Lu realized that he needed to take action. In order to save his family, he decided to become a qualified stay-at-home husband. He took care of the house, accompanied the children, and let his wife devote herself to work to earn more income. Through his efforts, the family finally got out of debt and let everyone have more happiness.

Mr. Li used to be a successful entrepreneur, but his company went bankrupt because the market change affected his business. In order to pay off his debts, he decided to move back to his hometown with his family and take charge of his own housework and children's education. After a year of hard work, his wife found a stable job and the family gradually got out of debt.

Ms. Wang was originally a company executive, but she was forced to resign due to poor performance of the company, and the whole family suffered financial difficulties. To cope with this situation, Ms. Wang decided to return to the family and take care of the children and do housework full-time. After a period of hard work, she managed to keep the family expenses within limits, and her son's grades improved greatly.

Mr. Zhang is in debt because his business has failed. To cope with the situation, he gave up his old job and returned to his family to take care of the children and do housework full-time. After more than a year of hard work, his wife earned a considerable income outside, and the family gradually got rid of the economic difficulties.

Mr. Wu was an entrepreneur, but his company didn't succeed because of the fierce competition in the industry. In order to pay off his debts, he decided to give up his career and return to his family to take care of the children and do housework all the time. Despite the difficulties, Mr. Wu persevered and eventually succeeded in helping the family out of debt.

Ms. Xu's company closed down and many of her employees became unemployed, and she was no exception. But instead of giving up, she chose to return to her family and take care of her children and housework full-time. After a year of hard work, his wife found a new job, the family's finances improved, and the children's grades improved dramatically.

In short, when people are in a state of bankruptcy, looking for family support is a good way to restore confidence and credit. We need to face reality bravely, be honest with family members and make plans together. Whatever role you play in your family, you can contribute to your family.

Social assistance and use of resources

If you are already in the midst of bankruptcy, don't give up hope, there are many social resources and assistance that can help you gradually get out of trouble. Here are some of the ways you can use the power of society to rebuild your life.

Actively apply for low-rent housing to reduce rent expenses

Applying for low-rent housing is usually one of the first choices for bankrupts, because rent expenses are one of the biggest fixed expenses each month. Apply for low-cost housing to the relevant government agencies to consult, understand the specific conditions and procedures for the application, and prepare relevant materials. Keep a positive attitude when applying and stick to the application to get a better application result.

Case:

Ms. Zhang is a family with a serious illness of the elderly, her family's financial situation is more difficult, can not afford high medical expenses, can not afford expensive housing costs. But fortunately, Ms. Zhang applied for the low-rent housing resources provided by the government and successfully obtained a house. From then on, she and her family finally lived a comfortable life. The government's low-rent housing program has not only helped Ms. Zhang, but also helped many groups like Ms. Zhang who have encountered bottlenecks, giving them new hope and courage to live.

Mr. Cheng is a retired old man, his income is not high, it is difficult to afford high housing costs. One day, a kind-hearted man introduced him to the government's low-rent housing program, and sent the application form. Mr. Cheng soon succeeded in getting a low-rent house to live in, and since then, his life has become easy and happy. The government's low-rent housing plan not only provides a guarantee and popularization for Mr. Cheng's life, but also allows many difficult elderly people like Mr. Cheng to get rid of their troubles and live a stable life.

Ms. Huang is a single mother. Her income is not high, but she has to bear high housing expenses. By chance, she learned about the low-rent housing program provided by the government and successfully obtained a low-rent housing in less than a month. Since then, her life has become more affluent and more confident in the future. The government's low-rent housing program not only helps ordinary families like Ms. Huang, but also helps those in more difficult circumstances, freeing them from the pressure and burden of life.

Mr. Liu is a business owner who has just gone bankrupt. His life is full of difficulties and challenges. In order to solve the problem of rental expenses, he applied for the low-rent housing scheme provided by the government and successfully obtained a house. Since then, his life has undergone earth-shaking changes, but also to his family brought a lot of hope and confidence. The government's low-rent housing program has helped battered entrepreneurs like Mr. Liu to bounce back, get out of trouble, and carve out their own upward path from a new starting point.

Mr. Zhang is a middle-aged man, due to investment failure, owed a huge debt, almost bankrupt. Later heard that the government has low-rent housing policy, he resolutely decided to apply, and finally got the government's assistance. Now, he lives in a nice low-rent house, paying only a little rent a month, saving money to pay off debts and slowly getting out of debt.

Ms. Wang is a housewife. After her husband lost his job, the burden on her family became heavier and heavier. She tried every means to relieve the pressure. Until one day, she heard that the government had a low-rent housing policy, and decided to apply, successfully obtained the government's help. Now, she lives in a good low-rent housing, rent is cheap, the pressure is reduced a lot, the quality of life has improved.

Mr. Li's family of four has been renting a small house, under great pressure. However, due to financial difficulties, he has been unable to buy his own home. Later, he heard that the government had a low-rent housing policy, immediately went to apply, and received government help. Now, his family lives in a new low-rent housing, rent is much cheaper, the burden is much lighter, life has become more comfortable.

Mr. Sun's family life is very tight, has been worried about renting money.

One time he learned about the government's low-rent housing policy from TV commercials and decided to apply. Through the government's review, he was eligible to apply and successfully obtained low-rent housing. Now, he only needs to pay a small part of the rent every month, saving a lot of money and improving his quality of life.

Ms. Zhao and Mr. family economic situation is very difficult, rental burden is heavy, living pressure is very high. One day, they learned about the government's low-rent housing policy and decided to apply. After a government investigation, they were eventually given low-rent housing. Now, they live in a comfortable and cheap low-rent housing, not only the rent is much cheaper, but also their financial burden is greatly reduced, and the quality of life has been improved.

Apply for unemployment benefits

If your bankruptcy is caused by unemployment, it is essential to apply for unemployment benefits. You need to submit an application to the employment department in accordance with the relevant policies, regulations and rules in your area, and provide your exact situation to receive assistance.

Case:

Xiao Li, a taxi driver in his late 40s, had to give up his taxi business because of the impact of the Xinguan epidemic. He applied for unemployment benefits, got through the toughest months, and then, with the introduction of a friend, found a new job and gradually worked his way out of debt.

Mr. Jia is a private enterprise owner, due to market changes, business difficulties, and eventually closed down. He applied for unemployment benefits, got through the toughest months, and then, with the help of friends, found a new job and gradually recovered financially.

Ms. Li is a professional manager. In recent years, due to the recession of the industry, the company's performance has been poor. Finally, the company closed down and she lost her job. Ms. Li applied for unemployment benefits, spent the most difficult months, and then found a new job with the help of social resources and human resources, gradually out of financial difficulties.

Mr. Zhang is a builder, because of policy changes and market changes, his business is no longer the same as before, eventually fell into the debt dilemma of millions of yuan. He applied for unemployment benefits, restructured his debt with government help, eventually turned it around and found a new job.

Ms. Wang, a construction engineer working in other provinces, was forced to return to her hometown during the Xinguan epidemic. She lost her job as the traditional construction industry was affected by the epidemic. She applied for unemployment benefits, got through the toughest months, and then, with the help of her connections, found a new job and gradually worked her way out of debt.

1. Xiao Zhang lost his job and had to apply for unemployment benefits

because he had no family to help him. He was actively looking for a job, took several trainings, and eventually got a job offer at an Internet company to regain his footing.

Ms. Li's husband was unable to work due to a sudden accident, and the family's economy was in trouble. When the staff of the residents 'committee learned about her situation, they helped them to apply for unemployment benefits in time and guided her to find new employment opportunities. Soon after, Ms. Li worked as a shopping guide in a shopping mall, improving her family's financial situation.

Mr. Wang lost his job because of the company's downsizing, and his family life became very difficult. With the help of unemployment benefits, he quickly adjusted his mentality and started his own business. After a long period of hard work, his signature noodle shop finally earned a reputation and completed its self-rescue.

Mr. Qian was unable to work due to illness during his employment, and his family became increasingly difficult. He resigned resolutely and applied for unemployment benefits, then got through the difficulties by actively looking for part-time workers and odd jobs, and finally found a stable job in a new company.

Ms. Xu was forced to resign due to family reasons and lost her financial resources. With the help of community volunteers, government workers and unemployment benefits, she gradually found a new job and improved her financial situation.

Apply for a poor student allowance for your child at school

If you have a child in school, you can apply to the school for a subsidy for poor students to reduce part of the burden. When applying, provide detailed information about your financial situation, which can help the school better understand your difficulties.

Case:

Xiaohua is an unemployed and bankrupt father who has run into a wall everywhere on his way to find a job. His wife takes care of the children at home and life is very difficult. Xiaohua's child is in junior high school. He likes studying very much, but poor families can't afford their children's tuition and living expenses. Therefore, Xiaohua began to look for ways to apply for school subsidies for poor students. After continuous efforts, Xiaohua finally successfully applied for the school poor students subsidy, the child can continue to complete their studies. In the process of learning, the child worked very hard and gradually became the best in the school. Xiaohua's family also slowly got rid of poverty and regained a happy life.

Mr. Li's company closed down and he became an unemployed man. He has a daughter who is in primary school. He always hopes that her daughter can study well and have a bright future. However, after losing his job, Mr. Li could no longer provide tuition and living expenses for his daughter, and his heart was very heavy. Mr. Li learned that the school had a bursary program, so he tried to apply. After a period of review, his daughter successfully received a grant. Mr. Li is very grateful for the help of the school, his daughter also because of the tuition and living expenses, happy to continue to go to school, daughter also in the school group activities outstanding performance, became a good friend of the students. Although the family is still in some financial difficulties, Mr. Li's family has hope and motivation to face the future bravely.

Miss Wang lost her job and took care of her two children at home. Her eldest daughter is very good at learning and art, but for financial reasons, she can't let her daughter participate in various trainings and competitions, which makes her and her children very sad. She learned that the school has a program to subsidize outstanding students, resolutely went to apply. After learning about Miss Wang's family's difficulties, the school paid close attention to her application. Miss Wang's daughter has received financial support and participated in various trainings and competitions to continuously improve her comprehensive quality and prepare for the future. Miss Wang's family also gradually stabilized, the eldest daughter became the pride of the family.

Mr. Sun is a teacher. His income is very low. He has several young children to take care of at home. His older daughter wanted to go to summer camp, but he couldn't afford it because of financial constraints. At the same time, his eldest daughter also suffers from a number of illnesses that require regular treatment. Mr. Sun heard that the school had a program to help families in need, so he went to apply. After the audit, his eldest daughter was awarded a place in the summer camp and a subsidy for regular treatment. Mr. Sun's eldest daughter took part in various activities in the summer camp, made many friends with her peers, and got more exercise and improvement in her hobbies. During the treatment, the child received timely medical help and recovered a little bit. Mr. Sun's gratitude to the school is beyond words.

Mr. Liu is a worker and his income is very low. His two children are studying and life is very difficult. His greatest wish is to provide better education for his children and give them a better future. Mr. Liu heard that the school had a program to subsidize poor families, so he went to apply. After a brief review, his child received financial assistance and the school provided adequate, safe and hygienic accommodation for the child. The child's academic performance has been greatly improved, but also more confident and happy. At school, his children met a lot of friends and had a wider range of interpersonal relationships. Mr. Liu's family still has difficulties, but his heart is full of hope and gratitude.

Mr. Zhang, a farmer living in a remote county in Sichuan Province, had a difficult family life after his wife died of illness. Mr. Zhang's income from farming and business could not support his education of two children alone, and his health began to suffer. But Mr. Zhang has always believed that as long as his children can have a good education, they will have a better future. Therefore, after constant inquiry and various attempts, Mr. Zhang applied for the government's subsidy for poor students for his children, and gave them enough support and encouragement. Now that Mr. Zhang's children have finished their studies, they are able to help the family out.

Ms. Li is a retired teacher living in a city in Shandong province. Her son needs to be hospitalized for a long time because of a sudden illness. The sum of her son's medical expenses and hospitalization expenses has forced Ms. Li to borrow a lot of money. Later, she heard that the government offered subsidies for poor students, and Ms. Li did not hesitate to apply for the program for her son, who was in high school. The money eased Ms. Li's burden and helped her son successfully complete his studies. Although the family debt did not disappear at once, Ms. Li also has more confidence and courage to face the future life.

Mr. Chen is a small farmer growing peanuts and green vegetables in a rural area in central Hunan. The family's financial situation is not good, especially when Mr. Chen's parents are old and need medical expenses, the burden is even heavier. But the hardest part was for Mr. Chen's eldest son, who was preparing for the gaokao, and his family could not afford expensive training. Funded by the government's subsidy scheme for needy students, Mr. Chen's eldest son was able to enroll in a course at a well-known training institute. A few months later, the child excelled in the college entrance examination and was admitted to a university. Although the financial pressure at home is still great, Mr. Chen has strengthened his confidence in working hard with his children.

In Shenzhen, Guangdong Province, Ms. Yang is a failed entrepreneur who has encountered many difficulties in running her own restaurant brand, which eventually led to failure. She, her husband and children were all in debt. However, for the future of herself and her children, Ms. Yang did not give up her dream, nor did she lose her care and education for her children. In order to allow her children to continue their studies and no longer be affected by the family's economic difficulties, Ms. Yang applied for a government subsidy for poor students for her children. In the process, the family's ongoing financial problems remain a serious problem, but Ms. Yang and her children, supported by love and hope, are gradually getting out of debt.

Mr. Qu, a migrant worker in a city in Hebei Province. He moved his family to the city in search of a better life, but after several years of hard work, he found it difficult to get what he wanted. The situation at home is also becoming more difficult every day, with frequent shortages and even arrears of daily living expenses. However, Mr. Qu still did not give up his efforts, in order to allow his children to continue to complete their studies, he is studying in junior high school son to apply for a poor student subsidy. This financial aid allowed the child to successfully complete his education. Although the debt problem of the family was not solved much, the family still moved forward with love and hard work.

When you are unable to pay for medical expenses, seek help from crowdfunding platforms such as water droplets

If you or your family need medical emergency, but you cannot afford the high medical expenses, you can seek help from crowdfunding platforms such as Droplet. This platform can help you get donations from others and ease your financial pressure.

Case:

Xiao Li, a farmer living in a poor mountainous area in Jiangxi Province, has a wife who is seriously ill and needs major surgery. However, due to the poor financial situation of the family, Xiao Li did not have enough funds to pay for medical expenses. Later, he thought of the water drop crowdfunding platform, released help information. In the end, with the strong support of netizens across China, Xiao Li raised enough money to operate on his wife, allowing her to successfully regain her life.

A young artist who has a rare disease and spends a lot of money on medical treatment is in critical condition. He and his family have raised part of the cost of treatment, but still need financial support. On the water drop crowdfunding platform, the crowdfunding project was launched, which was widely supported by caring people. After a difficult treatment, the artist finally recovered and created new achievements in art.

An 80-year-old man in Beijing needed surgery for a broken bone, but because his family was overburdened and his pension was not enough to support high medical expenses, he began seeking help online. After seeing it, netizens on the water drop crowdfunding platform extended a helping hand and raised enough money to help him complete surgery and rehabilitation. After learning that he could safely pass the operation, the old man deeply felt the help of the caring people and was very grateful.

A young mother needs long-term treatment for cancer, and her husband is an ordinary worker with a limited monthly salary. In order to raise enough money for their mother's expensive radiotherapy and chemotherapy, the couple traveled to relatives and friends, almost all their savings, and faced with the remaining high cost of treatment, they began to look for help. Later, they launched a crowdfunding project on the water drop crowdfunding platform. With the support of caring people, the couple had enough money to pay for treatment and recovered smoothly.

A young college student suffers from a congenital disease that requires expensive surgery at a young age. Because of his family's poor financial situation, he couldn't afford high medical expenses, so he launched a crowdfunding project on the drop-funding crowdfunding platform. With the attention of netizens, he successfully raised the funds needed for treatment and won the blessing of many netizens during the operation. After successful surgery, he has now recovered to a healthy state and is actively engaged in college studies and extracurricular activities.

Mr. Li is a healthy middle-aged man who suffered a broken pelvis in a car accident. After several surgeries and a long hospital stay, his medical bills have reached 300,000 yuan, and the long recovery process has left him unable to work. Under the threat of economic collapse, he made a call for help on the drop-funding crowdfunding platform. Soon, many sympathetic netizens came to his aid, donating money and sharing posts, so that Mr. Li finally raised enough funds, and the treatment and recovery went more smoothly than he expected.

Miss Wang is a young single mother with a small child who needs to be taken care of. Because of her family's financial difficulties, she did not want to go to the hospital to see a doctor in order to save money. She did not go to the hospital for treatment until she was unwell. She found that she suffered from serious illness and needed to pay huge medical expenses. In the face of high medical expenses, Miss Wang decided to publish help crowdfunding information on the water drop crowdfunding platform, which was responded by the majority of netizens who donated money to support and help Miss Wang and her children through the difficulties.

Mr. Song is a small businessman. After being poor due to illness, he bravely turned to several relatives and friends and water drop chips for help and crowdfunding. After getting the help of medical expenses, he decided to use his skills to start an independent business and lead the team to create products with market competitiveness. During the crowdfunding process, Mr. Song established close ties with the members of Droplet, and often exchanged experiences with them and shared his entrepreneurial journey. As a result, Mr. Song not only cured the disease, but also successfully owned his own business.

Mr. Zhang, a retired soldier, was injured in an accident and required medical treatment and long-term rehabilitation. Due to high medical costs and daily expenses, they face problems of debt and shortage of funds. Droplet crowdfunding platform also helped him. In addition to crowdfunding activities, it can also publicize and introduce its mission and value to the local area and provide practical help to more patients.

Ms. Liu is a mentally ill patient who needs a lot of medical expenses because of her complicated condition. Her family is very difficult at this time and cannot pay huge medical expenses. Therefore, she contacted her family, and soon her information was widely shared, and more and more netizens 'attention and support. After a period of crowdfunding, Ms. Liu fully recovered and her condition was well controlled. She and her family are also very grateful and moved by this kind and sincere help.

Set up a fundraising website to accept donations and promise to return

If you need a lot of donations to rebuild your life, you can set up your own fundraising website, accept donations from the public, and give back on your living conditions to build credibility and attract more donations.

Case:

Ms. Li's child was trafficked and she went bankrupt in the search. Due to lack of financial resources, she was unable to pay for the search. A volunteer saw her distress and offered to help her. Volunteers decided to build an electronic platform for finding abducted children and accepted donations from the public. Ms. Li finally found the child and took him home, and the help she received saved her from bankruptcy.

Mr. Zhang is a failed businessman who has been mired in huge debts and has fallen into a trough in his life. But he didn't give up. He thought of a good way to convince everyone. He set up a fundraising website and made public donations to raise money. Mr. Zhang promised to use the money to start his own business and repay his debts on time. Within a few days, his website received donations from many kind-hearted people, totaling 1 million yuan, and Mr. Zhang was finally able to get out of debt and restart his career.

Mr. Li is a young entrepreneur, due to excessive expansion led to the company's capital chain tension, facing the crisis of bankruptcy. He came up with the idea of setting up a fund-raising website on the internet to raise money for an emergency and promise to return it. He took the actual status quo of the company as the reason, and added his sincere attitude towards enterprise management, moved the hearts of thousands of netizens, the website raised 1.5 million yuan of funds. These funds were actually used to ease the company's business, and later the company stood up again and created better economic benefits.

Ms. Wang is a person who has always dreamed of opening a shop. She has a suitable location for a coffee shop in her home's West Lake District, but she has little money to complete the project independently. Until she set up a fund-raising website on the Internet and released information, promised to return investors, raised 1 million yuan of funds, and opened a beautiful coffee shop. She not only made investors return, but also created a unique brand, provided excellent service to local people, and achieved no small business success.

Seeking reports from media such as TV stations has drawn public attention

Public support and attention is a powerful force for the bankrupt. You can apply to the media, seek coverage, and use the power of the media to gain more social support.

Case:

Mr. Zhang is a small businessman who failed in business. He is in trouble because he is heavily in debt and owes huge debts. After many unsuccessful attempts to seek help, he decided to seek media coverage in the hope of attracting public attention. Through the power of the media, his story aroused widespread concern in society, and soon he obtained new job opportunities and successfully walked out of the debt crisis.

Ms. Wang was originally a senior medical practitioner, but her clinic recently closed down for multiple reasons. Faced with the sudden unemployment, Ms. Wang felt very helpless. She turned to television and other media for help, asking for coverage of her story. Through media exposure, she regained public recognition and support, and also got new job opportunities, successfully out of the predicament.

Mr. Liu, a teacher with 10 years of experience, lost his job after an accident and had to work in a small restaurant to make ends meet and pay off his debts. However, he did not give up, but took the form of interviewing the media and gained media attention. The media coverage caught the attention of the audience and brought him new career opportunities.

Mr. Li used to be a successful entrepreneur, but his business recently went bankrupt due to the poor economic situation in recent years. Mr. Li has increased the exposure of his story by seeking media coverage. Therefore, in front of the vast audience, Mr. Li has more opportunities to fight for new resources and start a new business. He also received social recognition and achieved successful development opportunities.

Xiao Wang is an independent entrepreneur in the restaurant industry. His shop went bankrupt because of the epidemic and mismanagement. He began to look around for new job opportunities, but never succeeded. Finally, he decided to ask the TV station for help and use the power of the media to attract people's attention. Through interviews and reports, he showed his diligence and honesty, and finally got a new job and finally got out of debt.

Xiao Zhang is a real estate agent. His business has been poor due to the depressed real estate market, leading to his financial situation getting worse and worse. He had been unable to pay off his huge debts and had fallen into despair. But, he heard that the network was looking for people with stories and decided to tell his story to the media. Through television coverage and asking for help, he got a new job offer and finally got through his financial crisis.

Xiao Li is a freelancer who specializes in attracting funding for businesses and organizations. However, since last year, his business has been affected, facing the risk of a broken capital chain. In order to get more opportunities, he began to promote his business through TV stations. Eventually, after much trial and error and asking for help, he won a tender for a major project that successfully solved his financial dilemma.

Xiao Liu is an English teacher hired by an international training center. Because of the impact of the epidemic, the center had to lay off most of its employees, including Xiao Liu. He felt very depressed and desperate and didn't know how to survive. However, his colleagues persuaded him to turn to the media in order to get attention from a wide audience. After his story was reported, an alternative training agency reached out to him and he was able to regain his job and fight again.

Xiao Zhao is the owner of a small factory, mainly engaged in wood products. However, due to fierce market competition and poor management, his factory was in a dilemma. At one point his department employees had to suspend work and he was in danger of going bankrupt. At a help-for-help meeting, he heard that television stations were looking for motivational stories, so he decided to share his predicament. To his surprise, a customer saw his story and offered him a large order. He quickly picked himself up, relaunched his business and remade his image.

In short, bankruptcy is not a permanent end, there are many social resources and assistance can help you gradually out of trouble. I hope you can face your situation positively and pursue your dreams bravely.

Consultation and communication with creditors

When a person goes bankrupt, communication and negotiation with creditors becomes particularly important. Here are a few tips to help bankrupts manage their debts and creditor relationships effectively and efficiently.

Be sincere

Make your difficulties known to creditors and be aware of your mistakes. This builds trust with creditors and makes it easier for both parties to reach a settlement. We need to understand the position and thinking of creditors. Creditors are also human beings, and they may have their own difficulties and needs. When negotiating and communicating with creditors, we cannot only consider our own interests and ignore the position of creditors. We need to respect each other and understand each other's thoughts and needs so that we can build a good relationship more easily. We need to conduct a comprehensive analysis and confirmation of our own situation. You need to know your income and expenses, as well as your debt. We need to communicate our difficulties clearly so that creditors understand our situation, making it easier for creditors to understand our situation. We need to choose the right time and place to communicate and negotiate with creditors. Consider the time and place of the creditor and choose a time and place acceptable to both parties for communication and negotiation. This allows both parties to communicate with peace of mind and achieve better communication results. We need to come up with a reasonable repayment plan based on our own financial situation and the situation of creditors. We need to adjust the repayment method and time according to our actual situation, so that creditors can accept it, but also can guarantee our quality of life. Only through sincere attitude, reasonable communication and clear plan, can we get out of the predicament as soon as possible. We should always be optimistic and believe that we can overcome this difficulty and move towards a better future.

Case:

Xiao Cheng is a small merchant, business is not doing well, owe a lot of debt. He was so stressed and confused that he didn't know what to do. Later, he decided to present his case to his creditors and ask for their understanding. After listening to him, creditors sympathized and found Xiaocheng very sincere, and finally decided to give him financial support and some business advice. Xiao Cheng was very grateful for their help and got out of debt step by step.

Xiao Li is a young man, working outside, because of his lack of financial ability, eventually led to his debt. At this point, he decided to talk to his creditors, explained his predicament to them, and the creditors were very considerate, helped him deal with his debts, and gave him some guidance on business ideas, which helped him start a new chapter in his life.

Master Wang, a construction worker, has less and less income due to his old age and infirmity, and he owes a lot of debt because his children's high school tuition fees cannot be paid. Later, he explained his situation to the creditors, who were very kind to help him through the difficulties and even gave him some financial support for his children to continue school.

Master Wang was grateful and got rid of the debt trap step by step with his own hands.

Ms. Zhang is an entrepreneur, because the external environment changes, affecting the company's operation, she has to face the debt dilemma. At this time, she decided to send a moving letter to the creditors, expressing her doubts, regrets and sadness. The creditors were deeply inspired and helped Ms. Zhang out of the debt quagmire. She finally moved towards a new path of success.

Mr. Liu is the boss of a company, because of the company's arrears and improper investment, resulting in his debt difficulties. At this point, he decided to apologize to the creditors and ask them for help. The creditors felt that he was very sincere, accepted his apology, gave him some preferential programs, and finally helped him successfully pay off all his debts. Since then, Mr. Liu has restarted his entrepreneurial road.

Xiao Li was an entrepreneur with his own small company, but because of economic reasons, his company went bankrupt. He owed a lot of debt, but instead of running away, he actively communicated with creditors. Creditors showed great sympathy and understanding when they heard of Xiao Li's plight. They agreed to give Xiao Li a grace period, along with appropriate financial support, to help him recover his business and eventually restart his career.

Mr. Zhang is an ordinary labourer. Due to poor hygiene, his family has suffered from some serious diseases. He had to go into debt to save their lives, but due to financial reasons, he failed to pay his debts on time and owed a lot of money. However, he has developed a good relationship with creditors through sincere communication and communication. Later, they agreed to pay the debt slowly if he bought some time, and gave him reasonable relief and support, which eventually helped him out.

Mr. Wang is a middle-aged farmer who needs to buy a new tractor to expand his business. However, due to the accident, his crops suffered a lot of damage, resulting in his inability to repay on time. In this case, he actively communicated with creditors and admitted his financial situation to them. The creditors understood his predicament and agreed to give him longer repayment periods and lower interest rates, helping him get back into business and eventually pay off his debts.

Ms. Tan is a young entrepreneur who started a new company. However, due to mistakes, her company suffered huge losses, resulting in her inability to repay her debts. At this time, Ms. Tan decided to solve the problem through timely communication and exchange. The creditors followed her advice and supported her in the process, helping her plan her finances, rebuild the company, and successfully get out of trouble.

Mr. Wang is a small shopkeeper who has been stolen while doing business, resulting in his inventory shortage. He needed to borrow money from the bank to buy more goods to meet his customers 'needs, but the loan amount was too small and the interest rate was very high. He couldn't pay his bills on time because of financial problems. He had the understanding and support of the bank in explaining his position to its creditors. Bank creditors agreed to his repayment plan and provided an appropriate extension within a reasonable time to help him get back into business and eventually out of trouble.

Repayment attitude should be positive

Show that you are willing to repay, but are currently unable to repay all of your debts. You can propose a repayment plan to gradually reduce the size of the debt and prove your repayment ability to creditors. What creditors need most is proof. Therefore, when communicating with creditors, be sure to show strong supporting materials to prove that you really have the ability to repay. These documents can include personal assets proof, income proof, debt list, etc. Only by having a positive repayment attitude, proving one's repayment ability to creditors and communicating with creditors sincerely can one obtain the opportunity of debt relief and debt settlement in the case of bankruptcy.

Case:

Xiao Wang is a freelancer, some time ago business downturn, resulting in a sharp drop in his income, unable to repay the previous debt. He was honest with his creditors and expressed his determination to continue paying. The creditors, aware of his difficulties and convinced of his good faith, eventually granted him a grace period and some relief. Xiao Wang spent three months actively making money and finally paid off all his debts.

Xiao Zhang's business mistakes caused the company to suffer heavy losses and he owed a huge amount of business loans. Faced with the grim situation, he showed his creditors his repayment plan, paying a certain amount of repayment on time every month in order to reduce the burden of debt. The creditors thought his plan was feasible, and through consultation, the two sides reached an agreement. Xiao Zhang did not slacken, earnestly fulfilled the repayment plan, and soon started a new business, and finally successfully paid off all the loans.

Xiao Li lost a lot of money because of gambling, resulting in his financial situation is very bad, even unable to pay debts. He tactfully explained his difficulties to his creditors and offered a detailed repayment plan. The creditors were well aware of the dangers of gambling, but seeing that Xiao Li had recognized his problems and taken action, they agreed to his plan. Xiao Li gradually paid off all his debts in the process of hard work and gradually recovered his financial situation.

Kobayashi's accident led to the instantaneous collapse of his family's economy, and he owed a large amount of medical expenses and other debts. At first, he tried to pay off all his debts by saving money, but soon found it impossible. So he spoke openly with his creditors about his problems and described in detail his actual situation and repayment plan. It can be heard that the creditor was very moved, agreed to his repayment plan, and continued to give him encouragement and support. Xiao Lin fought hard and finally succeeded in paying off all his debts.

Xiao Zhao's business has been developing smoothly, but due to the rising price of raw materials, his cost has increased a lot. As a result, his company began to crack under the pressure and began to take on a large loan. Faced with this situation, Xiao Zhao began to seriously review his management and showed his business plan and budget to creditors without reservation. The creditors, noting his enthusiasm and courage, agreed that his plan was very workable and agreed to his repayment plan. With painstaking efforts, Xiao Zhao quickly paid off all his debts and quickly resumed his original business profits.

1. Mr. Liu is a small businessman who has accumulated a certain amount of wealth for many years. But because of the investment failure, he owed a huge loan that could not be repaid in one lump sum. Mr. Liu actively contacted the bank and expressed his willingness to provide the property as collateral and actively repay the loan. The bank understood his situation and gave him maximum support. A few years later, Mr. Liu used his own efforts to pay off all the loans and smoothly walked out of the debt quagmire.

Miss Wang lost a lot of money by helping her parents invest, resulting in a huge debt. Through active communication with creditors, she expressed her willingness to repay regularly, handed over her membership card for borrowing, and issued an agreement to buy and sell real estate, so that creditors felt her determination to repay. Finally, Miss Wang paid off all her debts and got out of trouble smoothly.

Mr. Li owed a high debt due to the loss of funds. Through hard work and repeated communication with creditors, he expressed his willingness to gradually repay his debts and would do his best to find new ways to repay them. The creditors recognized Mr. Li's sincerity and efforts and gave him the support he deserved. A few years later, he successfully paid off all his debts and returned to his normal life.

Mr. Zhang lost his job due to illness, which led to a very difficult financial situation and owed a huge loan. Through frank communication with creditors, he expressed his predicament and hoped to extend the repayment period. The creditors understood his position and agreed to his request. After several years of hard work, Mr. Zhang finally succeeded in paying off all his debts and got rid of the trouble of debt.

Mr. Zhao invested in pursuit of high returns, but eventually failed and owed a large amount of debt. Through active communication with creditors, he said he would actively try to repay and attached his repayment plan so that creditors could see his sincerity in repayment. In the end, Mr. Zhao paid off all his debts, found new business opportunities and re-embarked on the road to success.

Communication should be appropriate

Fully absorb the negative emotions of creditors, actively seek solutions to problems, reasonably guide the emotions of creditors, and make communication smoother. When communicating with creditors, be sure to follow some basic rules, such as courtesy and respect. Don't use aggressive or emotional language or attitude. Try to express your views calmly and try to understand the creditor's position. Listen carefully to their point of view and respond to their questions to show that you are a willing partner. When people feel they are in a vulnerable state, they are likely to feel anger, fear, frustration and powerlessness. If these emotions are not properly alleviated, they will have a negative impact on negotiations and agreements. In this case, you need to ease their emotions with rational explanations and appropriate words. If you find that you can't calm them down, you need to calm them down a bit and start the negotiation again. If the creditor's mood becomes too emotional or too instrumental during the negotiation process, you can do something to guide it. This can be achieved by focusing on the end goal. You can clearly communicate your wishes to creditors and your reaction to any changes. This is to help creditors gradually adapt to the concept and seek consensus. When negotiating with creditors, it is recommended to opt for informal negotiations in a comfortable venue, which helps to build a relationship of trust and mutual support. By conducting the meeting in a pleasant and relaxed environment, you can express your solution more confidently and openly, while also giving creditors the opportunity to gain a deeper understanding of your point of view. If you can listen and understand the other person's point of view and make them feel that they are respected and cared for, then you can reach a win-win negotiation that you both need.

Case:

Mr. Zhang is a small business owner, because of poor management, he owed a lot of creditors a lot of debt. Mr. Zhang felt pressured by the calls and letters, but remained calm and explained his predicament to creditors. The creditors heard his feelings, understood his situation and agreed to give him a delay. Mr. Zhang worked harder and eventually paid off all his loans and got back on his feet.

Ms. Li is the owner of a small and medium-sized enterprise. She has encountered difficulties in the course of her business and has incurred a huge debt. Creditors came to demand their debts. They were very excited, cursing and threatening Ms. Li loudly. Ms. Li remained calm and said she would try her best to repay the loan. She established good communication with her creditors, who understood her predicament and gave her a grace period. Ms. Li kept working hard and successfully paid off all the loans.

Mr. Wang, the owner of a small and medium-sized enterprise, owed a large amount of debt after borrowing money from a bank because of a decline in sales due to changes in the market environment. Banks and other debtors have repeatedly called for debt, and Mr. Wang is under extreme pressure. He remained calm and offered the bank an installment plan. The bank staff understood his situation and agreed to his plan. Mr. Wang successfully paid off all the loans within the grace period and gradually got out of the debt quagmire.

Ms. Chen is a small restaurant owner, she encountered difficulties in the process of starting a business, and owed a debt. When creditors came to her, she kept her cool and explained her difficulties to them. The creditors understood Ms. Chen's situation and agreed to give her a grace period. Ms. Chen found her business picking up and worked hard to pay off all her debts.

Mr. Zhao is an entrepreneur who ran up a huge debt when he started his own company. Creditors came to the door to urge debts, emotional, threatening and questioning Mr. Zhao's ability and integrity. Mr. Zhao remained calm and conducted in-depth communication and exchanges with creditors. He provided creditors with detailed capital flows and company operations, and told creditors about his entrepreneurial story. The creditors heard his heart, understood his position and agreed to a grace period. Mr. Zhao continued to work hard and successfully paid off all the loans and regained his financial freedom.

The goal should be clear

In the process of communication, clear goals must be set and the goals must be achieved. Debt disputes can only be resolved by consensus. For the bankrupt, the goal is to reach a final agreement that will help you get out of debt disputes and get back to normal life. When setting the target, it is necessary to mainly consider the current economic situation of the other party, the requirements and interests of the creditor of the other party and the balance between the two parties. After setting a clear target, you can start to communicate with the creditor. In the process of communication, follow the principle of honest communication. If you can't reach an agreement, be honest and find other solutions. Otherwise, the agreement reached between the two parties is not sustainable. Negotiations will have to be held again. In the process of negotiation, we need to find a balance between the two sides. It is difficult to reach a consensus if you only focus on your own interests. Therefore, look for a middle ground to achieve a win-win outcome. When negotiating, pay attention to the feasibility of practical solutions. This avoids creating impractical protocols that can lead to more problems. Communicate honestly, look for areas where both parties can balance, and pursue practical solutions. Debt disputes can only be resolved by consensus.

Case:

Mr. Zhang was a bankrupt who failed in his business. He owed a huge debt and his life was in trouble. In order to get out of the financial crisis, he decided to negotiate with creditors and set clear negotiating goals for himself. While sticking to his bottom line, Mr. Zhang actively performed in the communication with creditors and finally reached a consensus. He worked hard to pay off the loan and restart his entrepreneurial career.

Ms. Wang has fallen into debt crisis because of a large loan due to business failure. In order to get out of the predicament, she decided to negotiate with creditors and set clear goals for herself. While sticking to her bottom line, Ms. Wang thought about different solutions and finally succeeded in reaching a consensus. Through hard work, she paid off her debts and regained her confidence.

Mr. Li is in trouble because he has a large debt due to the failure of his investment. He realized he needed to negotiate with creditors and set his own goals. During the negotiation process, Mr. Li kept calm, insisted on his bottom line, and finally reached an agreement with creditors to repay the debt in installments. He managed to get out of the loan mess.

Ms. Zhang is an entrepreneur who owes a large amount of money due to the failure of her business. She decided to negotiate with creditors and set her own goals. Despite the difficulties and setbacks in the negotiation process, Ms. Zhang stuck to her principles and moved closer to her goal. Eventually, she managed to pay off all her debts and restart her business plan.

Mr. Wang owed a large loan, and after the lowest point of his life, he decided to negotiate with creditors and set his own goals. Through grinding and discussion, he succeeded in reaching an agreement with creditors and obtained more relaxed repayment conditions. After several years of hard work, he finally paid off the loan, out of the debt quagmire, and regained a new life goal.

Don't be afraid to say no

Actively express their dissatisfaction and different opinions, and seek the understanding and support of creditors. However, be sure to express it in a reasonable way and not hurt the feelings of creditors. Don't be afraid to say no. During the negotiation process, you may encounter some creditors who make unreasonable demands or ask you to repay too short a period of time. At this point, you need to learn to refuse. After all, you are already bankrupt, and no matter how much you hurry, you can't catch up. Only according to your own burden can you gradually pay off your debts. If a creditor makes a demand that you can't accept or that you feel is unfair, you can express your dissatisfaction directly to them. Of course, you need to choose the right tone and manner so that creditors don't feel hurt or unhappy. Maybe you can find a more reasonable solution or buy more time to pay off your debt. You've done your best in bankruptcy, but the situation is beyond your ability. At this point, seeking the understanding and support of creditors is perhaps the most important step. You can explain your situation to creditors and let them know that you are actively working on a solution as well as paying off your debts. Perhaps this will help them recognize your difficulties and be more willing to give you some support and help.

Case:

Xiao Li is a bankrupt living in a small town in Henan Province. He ran up a debt because his business failed. His creditors threatened to sell his house and car to pay off his debts if he couldn't pay them off within a month. Xiao Li began to negotiate with creditors and insisted on his repayment terms. In the end, he and his creditors agreed that he could pay off the debt in two months.

In Fujian, a young bankrupt, Ms. Wang, ran up a huge debt because of a failed business. Creditors pressed her for repayment, threatening to detain her family and use hostages to force her to pay. Ms. Wang could not bear the pressure and began to express dissatisfaction. She then found a lawyer and appealed to the police. Eventually, she reached a settlement with her creditors and the debt was properly settled.

Mr. Zhang was the boss of a development company in Shanghai. Due to the market downturn, the company closed down and he owed a lot of debt. He began to negotiate with his creditors one by one for a repayment method that was in his favor. Mr. Zhang is confident that he can pay off his debts and is constantly trying to find a new job. Eventually, he managed to pay off all his debts and regain his financial freedom.

Mr. Zhao, the owner of a restaurant in Guangzhou, owed a lot of debt because his restaurant failed. He began to actively ask creditors for repayment terms, but almost every conversation did not go well. Later, Mr. Zhao hired a professional negotiator to help him negotiate with creditors. Through patient and meticulous negotiations, the delegates finally reached an agreement between the two parties, and Mr. Zhao successfully paid off the debt.

The owner of a small factory in Shandong Province was heavily in debt. He began negotiations with creditors, but with little success. Later, he found an outside intermediary to negotiate. Intermediaries help bosses repay their debts by offering different borrowing plans and repayment methods. In the end, the boss lived an affordable life and successfully worked his way out of debt.

Show the rascal properly

In the negotiation and communication, can be appropriate to show some rogue tendencies. That is, both hard and soft, to reach a settlement conditions. For some creditors, their main purpose is to make money. As a result, creditors often take advantage of personal difficulties and resort to rogue methods to force individuals to pay their debts. In this case, individuals can take some stimulating measures to make creditors feel that if they do not accept their repayment terms, they will face more serious consequences. In the communication with creditors, we should actively establish contact and trust with creditors. Sometimes, creditors may not be malicious, they may just worry that individuals will not be able to repay their debts, so they will take some enforcement measures. In this case, the individual needs to actively communicate with the creditor to convince the other party that he is sincere in repayment and establish a good trust relationship. Only then will it be possible to reach a positive agreement with creditors. Negotiating and communicating with creditors is a matter that requires caution and flexibility. It is necessary to use some rogue strategies reasonably to maximize the protection of their own interests, and at the same time actively establish good communication and trust relations with creditors, so that it is possible to reach the final settlement conditions through negotiation.

Case:

Xiao Ming is a bankrupt entrepreneur. During the economic crisis, his company went bankrupt. As his debts mounted, he became extremely anxious. He tried to explain his intentions and plans to his creditors, but they wouldn't listen to him. Xiao Ming finally decided to run away, creditors in trouble, almost collapsed. However, Xiao Ming struggled hard and finally paid off his debts, much to the surprise of his creditors. He was finally able to get out of debt.

Xiao Hong is a young professional woman who has run up a large debt in the process of opening a shop. She felt at a loss as to what to do with the debt. She tried to show her creditors her intentions and plans to repay, but they were not very interested in her plan. Xiao Hong began to adopt a strategy of both hard and soft, showing her seriousness and determination to creditors, allowing them to experience her ability and enthusiasm. In the end, she paid off her debts and showed her creditors her courage and determination to get out of debt.

Xiao Ming is the owner of an auto repair shop. His business was hit during the economic crisis and his shop was forced to close. His debts were mounting and he was desperate for business. However, he decided not to give up. He worked hard to show his creditors his willingness and plan to repay. Although creditors were unhappy with his repayment plan, they were impressed by his fortitude and determination. Finally, Xiao Ming paid off his debts, so that creditors believe in his determination and ability;He emerged from the mire.

Xiao Hong, an insurance broker, ran up a lot of debt while expanding her business. Her mind was in a whirl, but she was determined not to give up. She showed her creditors her intentions and plans for repayment, but they weren't interested. Xiao Hong began to take both hard and soft ways to prove her ability and enthusiasm to them, and to show her dedication and sincerity. In the end, Xiao Hong overcame the difficulties and paid off the debt, which surprised the creditors.

Make full use of legal knowledge to protect your rights and interests

During the bankruptcy process, you need to find a qualified lawyer if possible. A lawyer can help you understand the laws and regulations and make sure your rights are protected. At the same time, a lawyer can help you develop a workable repayment plan that can be negotiated with creditors. If you don't have this condition, you'd better search the relevant legal provisions and existing cases yourself. When communicating with creditors, be sure to communicate your case clearly. You should tell creditors that you are bankrupt, your income and liabilities, and that you are working to resolve the problem. In order to support your claim, you need to be prepared with any evidence that can prove your case. This can include records of income and expenses, as well as other financial information, and evidence of mortgages on various properties. In the process of negotiation and communication with creditors, we must fully understand the legal knowledge, protect their rights and interests, and ensure that creditors will not cross the bottom line.

Case:

Xiao Wang, a small-business owner, was short of money because of poor business management and had to face debt problems. However, he found that the contract between his bank and creditors was ambiguous, and through legal advice and lawyers 'advice, he eventually obtained a more reasonable repayment system through a series of complicated legal procedures, and was reborn after successfully paying off his debts.

Xiao Li is a successful businessman who invests a lot of time and money in his business. His business took a big hit because of improper authority and market changes. His debts include bank loans and loans from various non-bank financial institutions. Although his financial institutions and creditors once proposed to let him pay off his debts and hold bankruptcy liquidation, Xiao Li stood firm and insisted on going to court to protect his rights and interests, and obtained a more favorable repayment plan, successfully escaping the fate of bankruptcy.

Xiao Chen is a gambler, he regards gambling as entertainment, and once indulged in it. However, the debt from gambling was too great for him to continue to make a living. However, Chen did not give up, through his own efforts, he found a lawyer, with the help of the legal provisions involving gambling behavior, successfully removed gambling loans from his balance sheet, restarted his life.

Mr. Li, a long-unemployed construction worker, was in debt because he couldn't pay his medical bills. He studied the law, discovered that he had the right to apply to the government for medical assistance, and eventually succeeded in obtaining a large medical insurance settlement and struggling to pay off all his debts.

Ms. Zhang is a housewife whose husband lost all his property because of gambling and was in debt of millions of yuan. Part of Ms. Zhang's real estate was frozen because of her husband's dereliction of duty. She learned legal knowledge, used legal procedures to help her unfreeze her real estate, and finally paid off all her debts by selling her property.

Mr. Wang was a small trader who was heavily in debt after his business failed due to fierce competition and tight capital. He filed for bankruptcy reorganization through legal proceedings, successfully retained other business assets and obtained bankruptcy protection.

Ms. Liu, a young doctor, had borrowed money to buy a house but had difficulty repaying on time because of her low income. Ms. Liu actively sought legal aid, successfully suspended repayment through mediation and obtained a lower interest rate, thus successfully getting rid of the debt dilemma.

Mr. Yang is an SME owner who is in crisis due to business strategy and market changes. Mr. Yang actively studied legal knowledge and consulted lawyers, finally circumvented the pressure of vicious creditors, successfully reconciled with creditors and obtained financial support, so that the enterprise stood up again.

Keep the right to continue using the collateral as much as possible

If the collateral is involved in the process of communication and negotiation, the bankrupt must keep the right to continue using the collateral as much as possible. Collateral is often of great value to the bankrupt and must be handled with caution. If the right to use the collateral can be preserved, the bankrupt can restore his strength and repayment ability in the future through his own efforts and operation. In bankruptcy liquidation, creditors tend to give priority to obtaining collateral at the lowest possible price, thus taking advantage of the situation. Therefore, in the process of consultation with creditors, the bankrupt should list feasible schemes as far as possible so that creditors can obtain more benefits and protect their own survival and interests. In this process, the bankrupt needs to deal with relevant problems actively, legally and in compliance with the law, so as to protect his legitimate rights and interests and survival interests to the maximum extent. Don't be passive to escape, fate, it will make your loss even greater.

Case:

Mr. Li went bankrupt due to poor management and faced the situation of losing his family. However, he refused to give up, and through repeated negotiations with creditors, he finally got the opportunity to pay off all his debts at one time. He did not hesitate to sell his hometown and take out all his money to pay off his debts. Although sacrificing some benefits, he eventually succeeded in keeping the mortgaged house so that his family could continue to live in it.

Ms. Zhang owed a large amount of debt due to the business downturn, unable to repay, and creditors coerced and lured, even threatened to occupy her house. But Ms. Zhang didn't give up. She kept asking for help and held many negotiations with her creditors. Finally, with her conscious efforts, the debt was gradually paid off, and she managed to keep her house.

Mr. Wang suffered a great loss in his business and declared bankruptcy. He faced the pressure of bankruptcy, constantly looking for solutions, and finally, with a lot of effort, was able to keep the mortgaged home. "Debt is responsibility," he believes."Your family has to protect themselves."

Mr. Chung has been in debt crisis due to investment losses in the past, once faced with the mission of being pursued collateral. However, he did not give up, but actively communicated with creditors and proposed a "freeze" of collateral. The creditors agreed to this acquisition, which succeeded in reducing Mr. Zhong's debt burden and brought many lessons to his life.

Ms. Chen's high debt due to poor management has plunged the entire family into a desperate situation and is in danger of losing her home. However, through many negotiations, she constantly showed her sincerity to the creditor to solve the debt, and at the same time increased the amount of repayment, finally got the creditor's forgiveness, successfully saved her home, and gradually escaped the debt dilemma.

Xiao Wang is a freelancer, due to business downturn, his financial situation was in trouble. In order to make a living, he had to mortgage the only car he owned to a bank loan. However, due to a series of unpredictable factors, Xiao Wang has been unable to pay off the loan, and bank collectors have repeatedly threatened him to tow away his car. Faced with the threat of the bank, Xiao Wang chose to negotiate with the bank. After many communications, he finally succeeded in persuading the bank to delay the towing of the car until he paid off the loan, which gave Xiao Wang the opportunity to continue his own business. Eventually, he worked hard to pay off the remaining loans and got out of debt.

Young Li Mou in the process of starting a business into a financial bottleneck, in order to survive, he chose to mortgage his car to the bank, to friends and relatives to borrow money to make a living. But when a customer defaulted on his payments, his finances spiraled into a vicious circle until he ran up more debt than he could handle and bank collectors repeatedly came to have the car towed. At this critical moment, Li decided to solve the problem through negotiation and successfully persuaded the bank to delay the towing time of the car. Encouraged, Li strengthened his confidence, put more hard work to earn money back to repay the debt, and finally achieved the goal of paying off the loan.

Zhao, a middle-aged man, suffered heavy losses in the process of investing in real estate. He had to mortgage his car to maintain the normal operation of the investment project. But the battle didn't help him turn around his economic difficulties. Zhao's debt pressure was getting bigger and bigger, and bank collectors repeatedly urged him to repay his debts and prepared to tow away his car to clear his debts. Zhao realized that his situation was very serious, but he did not give up on himself. Instead, he negotiated with the bank staff and successfully postponed the date of towing his car. This gave Zhao time to remedy his investment losses and eventually paid off his loan.

A college student named Hooper, who started his own coffee shop after completing his studies, mortgaged his car to the bank to get money to keep the coffee shop running. However, his customer base was initially limited and could not meet the cost of the store. This forced him to apply to the bank for a loan. Unfortunately, the economy did not improve, Hooper's coffee shop business shrank, and his borrowing began to accumulate. At one point, bank collectors began to come frequently to collect his payments and prepare to tow his car. Through persistent efforts, Hooper succeeded in persuading the bank and received a temporary relief of funds. He began to take more effective action to lead his coffee shop out of the economic crisis, and eventually he paid off the loan and became one of the most popular coffee shops in the area.

Wang Mou, a small business owner, mortgaged his car and borrowed a large sum of money to expand his business momentum. Then something unexpected happened. His main client stopped working with him, and another competitor won market share. Wang borrowed a lot of money to make ends meet until a bank collector called and threatened to tow his car away. Faced with extreme difficulties, Wang chose to negotiate to ease his debt pressure and successfully obtained the understanding of the bank. Although he still had a lot of debts, he revived his business with hard work, proper planning and confidence in the future, and finally paid off the bank loan.

Actively use debt restructuring and transfer of debt to solve problems

Bankruptcy is one of the most difficult times in a person's life. Whether it is because of unfortunate health problems, family breakups, job losses, or economic collapse, creditors tend to appear immediately after bankruptcy, seeking repayment. Negotiating and communicating with creditors is important. Creditors need to know about your finances, and you need to provide them with information about your income, expenses, liabilities, and assets, as well as how you will manage your finances. Of course, this is not an easy task, as you tend to panic and panic when faced with bankruptcy. So, you need to be clear about your financial situation and do your best to build a relationship of integrity and trust with your creditors. Once you start communicating with creditors, regular follow-up is crucial. You need to update them on your finances, state your awareness of debt, or reflect on your repayment plan. Whatever your repayment plan is, you need to discuss it with your creditors to determine how to move forward. In the process of negotiation and communication, you can patiently explore the possibility of debt restructuring, or look for debt transfer programs. Debt restructuring is an option. This is a way to help borrowers restructure their debt so that their repayment schedules are more reasonable, while reducing variable interest rate costs. Although the negative impact of this negotiation and communication is small, we need to have a clear understanding of the reality and the amount of repayment we can accept. Debt restructuring is not free, so we need to be prepared and understand the associated costs before negotiating. Debt transfer is another option. This is a way to sell all assets and pay off liabilities in theory, but in practice this is not always the case. The debt transfer requires more costs because you need to pay additional stop payments and liquidation fees. These costs may be more than you can afford, so we need to negotiate additional compromises or negotiations to get more benefits.

Case:

Mr. Zhang is a middle-aged man who has failed in his business. His company is heavily in debt and facing bankruptcy. However, Mr. Zhang did not give up. He successfully implemented debt restructuring through negotiations with the company's creditors. He redoubled his efforts, paid off all his debts step by step, and finally brought about the company's business recovery.

Ms. Wang is a restaurant owner. As a result of poor management, her restaurant ran into huge debts. Ms. Wang did not give up. She successfully implemented debt restructuring through negotiations with debt institutions. By trying to control costs, improve service and introduce new dishes, she turned the restaurant around and paid off all her debts.

Mr. Li is a professional working in the construction industry. However, his company has been losing money due to changes in the market and has run up a lot of debt. Mr. Li did not give up. He successfully implemented debt restructuring through negotiations with the company's creditors. He continued to work hard to expand his business and work with multiple suppliers, eventually leading to the company's business recovery.

Ms. Zhang, a housewife, had to seek help in debt restructuring because of her family's debt problems. She successfully implemented debt restructuring through negotiations with debt agencies and started her business. She opened a small clothing store and worked her way out of debt by trying to control costs and constantly improve the quality of her products.

Mr. Luo is a financial practitioner, after an investment failure, his personal debt ballooned. Mr. Luo did not give up. He actively communicated with debt institutions, successfully implemented debt restructuring and began to re-plan his investment plan. He worked hard, learned more about finance, and got higher returns while controlling risk. In the end, he managed to pay off all his debts and achieved steady personal financial development.

Xiao Zhang is a young entrepreneur who has suffered several financial setbacks in the process of starting his business, which eventually led to the bankruptcy of his company. At this critical juncture, he decided to use debt transfer strategy to resolve his financial risks. He negotiated with his creditors to connect them to another well-funded acquaintance and transfer the debt to the acquaintance's company. After the successful transfer, Xiao Zhang not only eliminated the financial pressure, but also got some new investment channels, which allowed his new company to grow steadily.

Once a wealthy businessman, Xiao Li lost all his money in the economic catastrophe. While he was still trying to figure out how to deal with the debt, he received an unusual letter. The letter promoted a new type of investment portfolio and told him that he could use it as a way to relieve his financial difficulties. After some negotiations with the investment manager, Xiao Li's money returned to a steady return, allowing him to pay off his debts and get back on his feet.

Xiao Wang, a vagrant in a foreign land, fell into a very big debt trap in an accident, which made him fall into a great dilemma in his life. After many contacts, he found a job and began his arduous road of debt repayment. With his firm determination and enterprising spirit, Xiao Wang successfully paid off all his debts and allowed himself to return to the peak from the bottom of his life.

Mr. Zhang is an elderly retiree, but his children have not been able to support and take care of him. With the help of his friends, he learned some financial knowledge and obtained certain funds in a short time by means of loans and investments. Then he started a small business, paid off his debts, and spread the solid business to its fullest.

Xiao Wang, who was out of work, was in an extremely difficult financial situation because of his son's serious illness. To support his son's treatment, he had to borrow a lot of money. After a series of twists and turns, Xiao Wang successfully obtained a two-year interest-free loan in a negotiation with Western banks. The money allowed him to get enough money in two years to offset his existing debt and living expenses, and finally helped him through the difficult time in the hot summer.

In short, how to negotiate and communicate with creditors is a problem that people who have gone bankrupt must face and solve. In the process of negotiation and communication, we should maintain a sincere, positive and appropriate attitude, determine clear goals, and not be afraid to refuse, actively use legal knowledge to protect their rights and interests, and finally reach a settlement and solve debt disputes.

Conclusion: The Power to Succeed

I am glad to have written this Surviving Bankruptcy Guide. Because I know that this book will help many people, those who are trapped in the vortex of debt, lost confidence and courage. Bankruptcy is not the end of life, it is just a new beginning. In this book, I show you how to use your knowledge, skills, and judgment to better manage your finances, reduce your living expenses, and find new opportunities and ways to continue your struggle out of poverty.

The most important thing in this process is perseverance. No matter what you face, you must persevere. The power of perseverance is so

powerful that it can drive us to pursue our dreams even when our physical and mental strength is depleted. This power is true life force.

What we need to understand is that everyone has the opportunity to work hard and struggle. No matter what difficulties we encounter, we must move forward firmly, believe in ourselves and believe in the power of life. In this book, I share my own experiences and other people's stories, many of which I have painstakingly made up, but which I want to tell my readers. We can take control of our destiny, we can get better, we can succeed.

My message is not to gloss over difficulties or to say that everything is wonderful, but to tell you that difficulties are just a part of ordinary people's lives. We must learn how to face difficulties and find courage in difficult times. We need to see bankruptcy as the beginning of life, not the end.

Finally, I would like to emphasize once again the power of perseverance. Only by constant effort and struggle can we achieve what we want, whether it be wealth, security or happiness. So, whether you are in bankruptcy or on the road to success, keep going. You will find that the power to persevere towards success is endless.

Good luck with that.